Sport Management Cultures

This is the first book to address the link between culture and sport management. The aim is to demonstrate that culture profoundly affects how we research, teach and practice sport management. The book engages with the concept of culture both as an abstract analytical category and a set of specific beliefs and practices. It recognises that a single best way of managing does not exist; that the applicability of management theories may stop at national boundaries; and that fundamental cultural values act as a strong determinant to managerial ideology and practice. Culture makes the study of sport management interesting because it challenges many taken-for-granted assumptions about management, yet it reinforces our belief in the existence of common management problems.

The book offers a comprehensive review of the conceptualisations of culture and its relation with sport management by examining a range of issues: the emergence of multiculturalism as a policy issue; the impact of commonly shared cultural values within the fitness industry on managers and organisations behaviour; building cultural bridges in community sport organisations; cultural meanings attached to the consumption of Olympic merchandise, and culturally-informed interpretation through a reflective analysis of sport management texts.

This book was published as a special issue of *European Sport Management Quarterly.*

Vassil Girginov is Reader in Sport Management/Development at Brunel University. He has systematically researched and published in the field of sport management and development, and Olympism. His recent books include *The Olympics: A Critical Reader* (2010) and *Management of Sports Development* (Elsevier, 2008). He is also Executive Editor of Routledge 2012 Olympic Special Issue involving some 40 journals from a range of academic disciplines to be launched at the 2012 ICSEMIS Scientific Convention in Glasgow before the London Olympic Games.

Sport Management Cultures

Edited by
Vassil Girginov

Routledge
Taylor & Francis Group
LONDON AND NEW YORK

First published 2011
by Routledge
2 Park Square, Milton Park, Abingdon, Oxfordshire OX14 4RN

Simultaneously published in the USA and Canada
by Routledge
711 Third Avenue, New York, NY 10017

First issued in paperback 2014

Routledge is an imprint of the Taylor and Francis Group, an informa business

This book is a reproduction of *European Sport Management Quarterly*, vol. 10, issue 4. The Publisher requests to those authors who may be citing this book to state, also, the bibliographical details of the special issue on which the book was based.

British Library Cataloguing in Publication Data
A catalogue record for this book is available from the British Library

ISBN13: 978-0-415-60920-3 (hbk)
ISBN13: 978-0-415-75487-3 (pbk)

Typeset in Times New Roman
by Taylor & Francis Books

Disclaimer
The publisher would like to make readers aware that the chapters in this book are referred to as articles as they had been in the special issue. The publisher accepts responsibility for any inconsistencies that may have arisen in the course of preparing this volume for print.

Contents

Culture and the Study of Sport Management

VASSIL GIRGINOV

School of Sport & Education, Brunel University, Middlesex, UK

ABSTRACT This paper addresses the under-explored culture–sport management nexus and answers the question "why does it matter?". After reviewing the current culture debates, seven main aspects of culture and related underlying processes, which provide both the focus of and the milieu within which sport management operates, are identified, including (i) normative, (ii) innovative, (iii) *nomos*, (iv) singular and plural, (v) dialectic of system and practice, (vi) determined by production and (vii) political. The implications of these aspects for studying sport management are then examined, and research and practical recommendations are put forward. It is argued that by focusing on culture the field of study of sport management changes. The researcher is no longer interested only in what makes people participate in sport, watch a game or how organizational structures are designed; rather, s/he is seeking to understand the underlying cultural processes that drive and facilitate people's and organizations' behaviours in sport. Sport management is interpreted both as a representation of the symbolic cultural system within which it operates and as a means of actively shaping this system. Sport managers are seen as mediators of meaning; sport organizations as institutions for socialization, acculturation and control. A call is issued for scholars working in this field to promote greater cultural sensitivity.

Introduction

The main goal of this special issue is to address sport management from a cultural perspective. The culture–management nexus has long been established both theoretically and empirically. Until the early 1970s the study of culture was the preserve of anthropology, and management writers had to borrow insights from it to explain differences in management styles and effectiveness across various cultures. Gradually, other disciplines, such as sociology, psychology and linguistics, started to embrace the concept of culture. As a result, there has been a proliferation of theoretical perspectives and a growing number of academic peer-reviewed journals. At the time of writing a basic search of the British Library collection returned 229 culture-related journal titles.

Despite the apparent realization of the importance of culture, the culture–sport management nexus, however, remains a relatively unexplored territory. A legitimate question to be asked at this point is why does it matter? It is the purpose of this collection to demonstrate that culture profoundly affects how we research, teach and practice sport management. Oftentimes claims are put forward that sport represents a global phenomenon and a universal language, which has led to temptations to promote universal principles and practices for managing sport. Although commentators agree that managers world-wide share common problems, it has also been recognized that a single best way of managing does not exist; that the applicability of management theories may stop at national boundaries; and that fundamental cultural values act as a strong determinant to managerial ideology and practice (Hofstede, 1996; McGuire, O'Donnell, Garavan, Saha, & Murphy, 2002; Mwaura, Sutton, & Roberts, 1998; Richman, 1977).

In 2006 the *Academy of Management Journal*[1] surveyed its editorial board members and asked the question "what makes management research interesting, and why does it matter?" (Bartunek, Rynes, & Ireland, 2006). It is worth noting that two of the top three most interesting articles were concerned with culture (Barley, Meyer, & Gash, 1988; Dutton & Dukerich, 1991). Culture makes academic research interesting because it challenges many taken-for-granted assumptions about management, yet it reinforces our belief in the existence of common management problems.

This special issue of *European Sport Management Quarterly* engages with the concept of culture both as an abstract analytical category and specific beliefs and practices—hence culture in plural in its title—"Sport Management Cultures". The intention is to demonstrate the explanatory power of culture for the study and practice of sport management. The approach to culture taken here is different from the field of cultural studies of sport. The main concern of cultural studies is with sport as a form of cultural practice with its own relatively autonomous field of effects aimed mainly at liberating human potential through critical reflections on social conditions and power relations. When put together, practice and effects produce a conjunctural identity articulated with a network of relations (Andrews, 2002; Andrews & Giardina, 2008). This collection is also different from the field of cultural history of sport. In a recent special issue of *Sport in Society* on sporting cultures, Hughson (2009, p. 1) explained that this field is "especially concerned with how communal passions and feelings of people have been so strongly invested as to make possible a discussion of the *making* of sporting cultures". However, both cultural studies and cultural history provide useful analyses of sport as a historically evolved form of cultural practice which has shaped personal and group identities, as a configuration of power relations and forms of political and practical knowledge. Thus, these two fields of study should be seen as complementary and with particular relevance for sport management: both offer valuable insights into the cultural, social, political and economic milieu within which sport management theories and practices take place.

This special issue builds on the work of other sport management scholars. In particular, it responds to the call made by a special issue of the *Journal of Sport Management* (JSM) on "Promoting Critical and Innovative Approaches to the Study of Sport Management". Although not explicitly, Amis and Silk (2005) argued for more culturally-informed research by encouraging fellow sport management students to move away from positivistic research grounded in a Western epistemology which has dominated and continues to dominate the field (see also Quarterman, Hwang, Han, Pitts, Jackson, & Ahn, 2010). The contributions to the JSM volume provide examples for a range of research strategies, including participatory research, narratives and comparative studies, all of which take account of culture.

Cunningham and Fink (2006) edited a special issue of the *Journal of Sport Management* on "Diversity Issues in Sport and Leisure". They called for greater sensitivity about gender and ethnicity as key cultural characteristics. A welcome addition to the literature has been *The new sport management reader* (Pope & Nauright, 2009) which addresses a wide range of epistemological and emerging issues. The editors noted the utter, cultural disconnection of the North American college sport outside the USA and the effort to globally conceptualize sport management cultures. As Pope and Nauright (2009, p. xviii) stated "the key concept underpinning this effort is the world 'culture'".

This introductory article sets the scene by interrogating the link between culture and sport management and is divided into three sections. The first section offers an overview of the culture debate and its relevance to the study of sport management. The second section develops an argument for interpreting sport management as a specific cultural system of meaning and practice. Finally, the paper introduces the structure of the special issue.

The Culture Debate and its Relevance to Sport Management

Acknowledging the complexity of the culture concept is more than a statement and reflects truly complex and entangled historical, political, economic, religious and linguistic realities. As Eagleton (2000, p. 2) observed "the Latin root of the word 'culture' is *colere*, which can mean anything from cultivating and husbandry to worshiping and protecting". Stocking (1966) examined the culture concept in historical perspective and suggested two different usages of the term "culture"—the humanist and the anthropological. These two interpretations of culture have important implications for our understanding of the world and sport in particular. Stocking (1966, p. 868) commented that "anthropological 'culture' is homeostatic, while humanist 'culture' is progressive; it is plural, while humanist 'culture' is singular. Traditional humanist usage distinguishes between degrees of 'culture'; for the anthropologist, all men are equally 'cultured'. The humanist interpretation of culture became associated with the "civilization process" with which the West has justified its attempts to conquer the world. The notion of civilization was useful because it played down national differences, whereas culture highlighted them. Modern sport, including its bureaucratic forms of organization, rules, regulations and striving for efficiency, has largely been established through this process. It is worth recalling the words of Thomas Arnold, headmaster of the elite English school of Rugby and a founding figure of modern sport: "races unable to absorb European culture would dwindle away and, in the end, become extinct" (cited in Powell, 1995, p. 203). The role of sport was to train the future world leaders destine to fulfil this prophecy.

In contrast, the anthropological usage of the term suggests that the essence of the culture idea is learned behaviour which is socially transmitted and cultivated over time, and which serves as a main determinant of human behaviour. The vast majority of literature on national and organizational culture has been informed by this essentialist interpretation. Subsequently, studies on sport organizations' culture have proceeded from the premise that organizational members' values determine their behaviour, and have devised various instruments to measure it (Choi & Scott, 2008; Colyer, 2000; Smith & Shilbury, 2004). Another stream of sport management studies and practices within the anthropological interpretation has recognized the plurality of human nature and concentrated on conceptualizing and managing cultural diversity (Chelladurai, 2001; Cunningham, 2007). For example, Sport England (2002) has published a "No Limits" equality policy which recognizes diversity in its various forms, makes a commitment to promote an inclusive sport and encourages all sport organizations to adopt this policy and to nurture a true culture of diversity.

In a comprehensive review of the conceptualization of culture, despite the variety of disciplines and interpretations, Groeschil and Doherty (2000) contended that many of the existing definitions are based on two early anthropological ones proposed by Kluckhohn and Strodtbeck (1961) and Inkeles and Levinson (1969). The essence of both definitions is that they "aimed to identify common human problems which are shared by all human groups, but which are measured in different ways" (Groeschil & Doherty, 2000, p. 13). Those universally shared problems emerge from the relationships that people form with other people, and their attitudes to time, activities and the natural environment.

Morden's (1999) extensive management review of models of national culture examined their relevance to the study and practice of management. He advanced further the belief that "it is unrealistic to take an ethnocentric and universalistic view towards the principles and practice of management as they are applied in other countries and other cultures" (p. 20). Morden identified three types of cultural models, single (Hall, 1976, 1990; Lewis, 1992), multiple (Hampden-Turner & Trompenaars, 1993; Hofstede, 1980; Lessem & Neubauer, 1994) and historical-social (Bloom, Calori, &

de Woot, 1994; Chen, 1995; Seagrave, 1995). Adler (1986) offered a useful typology of management studies involving culture and identified six different research approaches, including parochial, ethnocentric, polycentric, comparative, geocentric and synergistic.

When informed by positivist epistemologies, both the humanist and anthropological usages of the term culture have resulted in its reduction to a variable, which once conceptualized could be operationalized, measured and evaluated. Consequently, there has been a myriad of operationalizations of culture (Alvesson & Sveningsson, 2008; Holden, 2002) and organizational culture (see Jung, Scott, & Davies, 2009 for a comprehensive review of instruments). But culture is more that a variable or a "side dish" (Trompenaars & Hampden-Turner, 1997). "Culture is ordinary: that is the first fact", wrote Williams (1958, p. 6). He continues,

> every human society has its own shape, its own purpose, its own meanings. Every human society expresses these, in institutions, and in arts and learning. The making of a society is the finding of common meaning and directions, and its growth is an active debate and amendment under the pressures of experience, contact, and discovery, writing themselves into the land (p. 6).

Writing in the age of computers some 25 years later, Hofstede (1984, 1993) defined culture as the mental programming or the software of the mind. The second equally important fact, according to Williams (1958, p. 6), is "the testing of these in experience, the making of new observations, comparisons and meanings". Therefore, "a culture has two aspects: the known meanings and directions, which its members are trained to; the new observations and meanings, which are offered and tested" (Williams, 1958, p. 6).

From Williams' point of view sport management could be seen both as ordinary and innovative. This is because the management of sport performs the double task of reproducing and reinforcing certain social practices, such as promoting national identity, developing character and teaching moral norms on the one hand, and challenging people's perceptions and behaviour by encouraging them to embrace new physically active lifestyles and by constantly pushing human and technological boundaries in the quest for sporting excellence, on the other.

It follows that various sport management conceptualizations and practices represent examples of specific cultural patterns bounded in space and time. But research also needs to be able to deal with culture at an abstract level, or what Sewell (1999) called a category of social life. Therefore, culture can be interpreted in two senses—singular (an abstract category) and plural (a bounded world of beliefs and practices). The latter sense implies that culture becomes identifiable, so we can speak of a Western or Asian style of sport management, or football, organizational and snowboarding cultures. In the former sense, culture, as a category of social life, has been conceptualized in a number of different ways, but most approaches invariably have recognized it as dialectic of system and practice. As Sewell

(1999, p. 47) noted, "System and practice are complementary concepts: each presupposes the other. To engage in cultural practice means to utilize existing cultural symbols to accomplish some end".

The notion of the culture system comprising symbols and meanings has been systematically developed in the works of Geertz (1973). It was introduced to distinguish specifically between two other systems—the social system composed of norms and institutions, and the personal system, concerned with people's motivation. In particular, he examined religion as a cultural system in trying to understand how its ensemble of symbols and the practices in which they are employed mutually sustain each other. According to Geertz (1973, p. 90) "religious symbols formulate a basic congruence between a particular style of life and a specific (if, most often, implicit) metaphysic, and in so doing sustain each with the borrowed authority of the other". Borrowing from Geertz's complex analysis to understand sport management as a symbolic system would suggest attending to two complementary symbolic orders of which it is composed—an ethos ("a people's tone, character, and quality of life, its moral and aesthetic style and mood") and a world view ("their picture of the way things in sheer actuality are, their most comprehensive ideas of order") (Geertz, 1973, p. 89). Various notions of management, such as Total Quality Management (TQM), High Commitment Management (HCM) and New Public Management (NPM), as well as sport organizations' social responsibility, code of ethics, and equality, child protection and anti-doping policies, are examples of ethos and world views, as they are reflective of the different ontologies that organize people's life and offer solutions for putting those matters in order. Maruyama's (1984) comparative analysis of Western, Asian and African concepts of management vividly demonstrates this point.

Management concepts, therefore, do not represent a neutral and technical set of activities, performed by neutral technical experts. As Flynn (1997, p. 41) argued, "management techniques and styles are themselves political" and form the core of "managerialism" as an ideology. Clarke, Gewirtz, and McLaughlin (2000) contended that managerialism defines a set of expectations, values and beliefs. Managerialism is thus a normative system with its own parameters as to what counts as valuable knowledge. Who knows what, and who is empowered to act as the consequence, are significant issues for this inquiry. Similar to the role of religion, sport management doctrines and practices also seek to align different groups of people's conception of real life with their conceptions of the appropriate way to live through the medium of sport. Sport management, as a concept and a set of practices, reflects the interplay between the two symbolic orders—ethos and world view. Whether seen in the context of elite athletes' development, recreational participation or sport fandom, sport management aspires to assert an ideal image of self-realization with a particular physically active style of life. One needs only to consider the relationship between the two symbolic orders in some Arab or Asian cultures to understand how the ethos impacts on the world view in a very different way from the West, thus providing a whole new meaning to sport management. Physical activity is seen as inappropriate for women in the former and as a distraction from the all-important mental domain by the latter culture.

Hong's (2009) dynamic constructivist approach to culture lends support for the above interpretation of sport management. Hong (2009, p. 4) defines culture as "networks of knowledge, containing learned routines of thinking, feeling, and interacting with other people, as well as a corpus of substantive assertions and ideas about aspects of the world". Moreover, Hong's approach specifically identifies the causal potential of culture, which "resides in the activation of the shared cultural knowledge, which brings about affective, cognitive and behavioural consequences" (p. 4). Seen from a dynamic constructivist perspective, sport managers are in the business of utilizing and developing networks of knowledge to promote specific consumer participatory behaviours. In short, sport managers become mediators of meaning. They constantly draw on symbolic systems, such as sport role models, national, club and hall mark events' insignia, and more holistic portrayals of a healthy way of life, in order to promote certain desirable behaviours. The work of Smith, Petersen, and Wang (1996) provides useful insights into the meaning of the production role of managers in different cultural environments.

Culture is also contradictory and contested. Culture is deterministic as it moulds us through traditions, customs, rituals and language, but we do not remain passive in the process and equally shape our own culture by engaging with it and using it as a resource. Culture provides and prescribes norms and values, but people constantly challenge the existing and establish new norms and values as well. Cultural norms, traditions, language and shared values are critical for holding society together, thus they act as a factor of social stability which ensures homogenization of meanings and behaviours. However, culture always implies the idea of the other and, as Kopytoff (1986) argued, the essence of culture is discrimination, which runs counter to homogenization. Individuals and groups constantly try to assert their identities by distinguishing themselves from others. Culture, therefore, bears particular relevance to politics and management, as it possesses cohesive and divisive social powers. Because of that, as Eagleton (2000, p. 26) pointed out, "culture comes to prominence intellectually when it becomes a force to be reckoned with politically".

Cultural diversity, or otherness, in its various forms—from gender to national identity to sexual orientation—serves as a source not only for academic studies, but equally for political debates, practical policies and national and international legislations. There are ample examples from the field of sport illustrating the interplay between academic debates on culture and practical policy issues: the constitutions of most sport organizations specifically recognize ethnicity, gender and age as determinants of participation in sport and call for equality; sport marketers have increasingly been employing ethnographic methods to study their customers in order to offer the most culturally relevant products and services; multiculturalism, although variously interpreted, is also a well-established characteristic of national sport policies in many countries. Eagleton's point, however, raises a more fundamental issue about the relationship between culture as a concept and practice. This point is well elaborated by Barley et al. (1988) in their study on cultures of culture, which was identified earlier as one of the top three most interesting papers by the *Academy of Management Journal*. In examining the flow of influence between two subcultures (academics and the management community), contrary to the conventional assumption which sees academic knowledge as an important source of empirical principles, the authors concluded that "conceptual and symbolic influence flowed in only one direction: from practitioners to academics" (p. 52). It follows that sport management thoughts draw on culturally meaningful practices. Indeed, as Geertz (1973, p. 5) commented, "if you want to understand what science is, you should look in the first instance not at its theories or its findings, and certainly not at what its apologist say about it; you should look at what the practitioners of it do".

Despite the multiplicity of conceptualizations, commentators generally agree, as two of the earlier influential anthropologists Kroeber and Kluckhohn (1952, p. 41) pointed out, that the essence of the cultural process is "the imposition of conventional form upon the flux of experience". Watson (1994, p. 20) also argued that "culture can be understood as a human creation which helps human beings avoid the dark abyss of disorder and chaos into which they might otherwise fall. The cultures we develop also assist us in making decisions". Similarly, as Clegg and Palmer (1996, p. 3) put it, "management is a process of social control", which "ideally in so many of its own representations, confers order, reduces uncertainty; it is the capacity to render the uncertain manageable, to conquer space and time with strategic direction ...". Writing on the social anthropology of management, Linstead (1997, p. 87) made the culture–management nexus explicit: "management is a social process, involving negotiations and construction of meaning to get things done". He also suggested that "management is differentially defined at the operational level" (p. 88), that is, at the level of practice. Thus, from a cultural point of view sport management, as a bounded world of beliefs and practices, should always be interpreted in plural, and as embedded in local systems of symbols and meaning.

Culture and management, therefore, are *nomos*-building activities—both strive to create *nomos*, order, out of chaos, to use Berger's (1973) phrase. As Todorova (1997, p. 116) explained, "The human attempt to give meaning and order to the world has been called a 'nomos-building activity', involving the process of typification which confers knowability and predictability". Cultural meanings thus, guide thinking, feeling and acting. Culture and management are descriptive and normative—ultimately both seek to reduce uncertainty and to confer order, hence they are not separate but closely intertwined entities. Various interpretations of sport management are cultural constructs underpinned by core assumptions and values held by members of professional communities in different countries. These values arise from social, cultural, organizational and ethnic dimensions. We cannot fully comprehend why managers act the way they do without considering the meaning they ascribe to their actions and the environments. It is equally important to recognize that culture and management are mutually constructive. Apart from being *nomos*-building activities, as Williams (1989, p. 8) noted, "a culture must be finally interpreted in relation to its underlying system of production". Management, both as a discourse (i.e. body of knowledge and curricula) and a performative activity (i.e. skills and tool kits), assumes the role of a major tool in the production and reproduction of sport as a particular form of physical culture. Expanding on this point will take us into the realm of cultural studies, but it is worth quoting Carrington's observation (cited in Andrews & Giardina, 2008, p. 402), which makes the link between culture and production clear. He specifically connected the dialogic process within a Nike commercial to "the exploitative economic production of the shoes themselves in Southeast Asia, through to their consumption in the deprived inner-cities of the West, and the meaning this produces".

In a recent special issue of *Management Decision* on "Taking Sport Seriously", Chadwick (2009) made an attempt to project the sport management research agenda for the twenty-first century. He identified uncertainty as the fundamental basis of sport and argued that the challenge for sport management scholars "now is to really start thinking about how uncertainty impacts upon how we research, study and practice sport management" (p. 193). Chadwick suggested eighteen areas of sport management affected by uncertainty for future research consideration, but culture was not one of them. As argued, culture's main function is to create order and to avoid uncertainty, which places it at the heart of sport management studies.

In summarizing the culture debate, seven main aspects for the study of sport management can be identified (Table 1).

1. Culture is an organized, logical, shared and learned system which is transmitted and accumulated over time, thus it is deterministic and normative.
2. Culture is also an innovative and constantly evolving system and a site for testing new observations and meanings.
3. Culture's main function is to create *nomos* or order so it can ensure the survival of a group of people.
4. Culture can be interpreted both as an abstract category (singular) and a bounded world of beliefs and practices (plural).
5. Culture represents dialectic of system and practice where each presupposes the other.
6. Culture is ultimately defined in relation to the underlying system of production.
7. Culture has political significance.

Related to those aspects of culture are seven underlying processes which provide both the focus of and the milieu within which sport management operates. It should be noted that those aspects and underlying processes of culture are interrelated and mutually enhancing. There are also different

Table 1. Key aspects of culture, underlying cultural processes and their implications for understanding sport management

Culture seen as	Underlying processes	Sport management implications
Normative	Socialization and acculturation of people in and through sport	Managers as mediators of meaning
Innovative	Making new sport cultures	Change management
Nomos	Social control and group survival	Common management problems—specific solutions
Singular and plural	Singularization and homogenization of sport cultures	Brand, organizational culture and diversity management. Concerns with social inclusion, equality and how to make policy sense out of a universe of diverse cultures while preserving social control. Researchers and managers need clear understanding of culture at abstract level in order to deal with differences in various environments
Dialectic of system and practice	Systemic interaction between symbols and practical actions	Employing mixed methodologies to capture the system–practice dialectic
Determined by production	Socio-economic organization of sport	Recognition of sport management as a political discourse and designing interventions and curricula accordingly
Political	Political recognition of cultural issues/multiculturalism	New forms of sport governance

from Hofstede, Neuijen, and Ohavy (1990) six characteristics of culture including a seventh characteristic added by Alvesson and Sveningsson (2008). The next section uses these seven aspects of culture and their corresponding underlying processes as pointers to unpack sport management from a cultural perspective, while concurrently considering some research and practical implications.

Sport Management: a Cultural Perspective

Culture as an Organized, Logical, Shared and Learned System

The normative and deterministic aspects of culture form the core of the related processes of socialization and acculturation. Allison (1982) made a convincing argument for studying the interrelationships between culture and socialization in the context of play, games and sports. She showed that historically, sport has been linked to the process of socialization, as it teaches children the ideas, rules and expectations which guide their behaviour and the behaviour of others. The socialization process, therefore, represents the mechanism by which such learning, or transfer of explicit and implicit values, occurs. From a cultural point of view sports are both patterns of behaviour and patterns for behaviour. Despite claims for the emergence of a global sporting monoculture (Donnelly, 1996), sports remain idiosyncratic, as people attach different meaning to them. As Allison (1982, p. 13) stated "games come to represent the patterns of behaviour of the culture in which they are found".

The important take away for senior sport managers is that they need to consider their job not only as ensuring the survival of the organization, but essentially as steering the socialization process that takes place in and through sport. This entails interpreting sport managers, coaches and celebrities as socializing agents (i.e. significant others), sport clubs and venues as social situations where social interaction takes place, and the personal attributes of people consuming sport as the three key elements of the socialization process. The ultimate aim of this process is to make people adopt a desired role of a sport member, participant and customer. Often, sport managers tend to underestimate the cultural difference between themselves and the people with whom they are dealing. In order for sport managers to secure the survival of their organizations they try to influence their customers and members symbolically and conceptually. For Barley et al. (1988, p. 27), similar efforts amount to acculturation, which they defined as "the process by which the beliefs and practices of one community diffuse across the boundaries of another and subsequently alter the second community's practices and interpretations". More specifically, those authors examined the role of language through which members of a culture encode and communicate, and suggested that "being a member of a different culture is tantamount to being a member of a different speech community" (p. 27). This statement has significant implications for sport managers as it presents them as constructors and mediators of meaning who draw on various symbolic systems to communicate certain messages.

Culture as an Innovative and Constantly Evolving System

The innovative aspect of culture suggests that sport managers are equally in the business of constantly interpreting, accommodating and changing the cultural world around them. On a more global level, the case of extreme sports, such as mountain biking and snowboarding, among others, is illustrative for the making of new sporting cultures. Originally, those activities emerged as a way of life and a form of resistance to the mainstream sport culture of particular groups of young people who were searching for alternative ways of expressing their identities and interacting with the world. Gradually, with the help of various management strategies, those sports become institutionalized and through the medium of the Olympic Games homogenized into a global sporting culture. But sport managers are also offering and testing new cultural products and services all the time—from equipment to activities, competitions and technology-aided ways of experiencing sport.

Offering and testing of new cultural meanings and practices require sport managers to be concerned with change management. In addition to responding to external social, political and economic pressures for adjusting organizational structures and practices, sport managers need to recognize that cultural change entails giving proper attention to the relationship between visions of management interventions and people's subjective perceptions of it. From a cultural perspective change management has to focus on the impact of management visions and actions on the reconstruction of subjectivity. By their very nature sport management interventions aim at improving people's wellbeing. However, improvement is a subjective concept, and subjectivity is determined by identity and culture.

Culture as Nomos

The *nomos* aspect of culture is mainly concerned with the process of social control and group survival. Historically, sport has always been used as an instrument for nation building through its potential to ensure military preparation, to train disciplined subjects, and to provide a meaningful form of leisure consumption. Increasingly, the management of sport has been concerned with preserving the social order and holding societies together. This is part of what Pitter and Andrews (1997) called "the social problem industry", where nationally and internationally sport has been employed to tackle anti-social behaviour, public health issues, multiculturalism and peace.

Commentators agree that despite cultural differences, there are common management problems but managers differ in how they solve those problems. Various management approaches are representative of the cultural choices made by people, but ultimately they serve as a means for ensuring social control and organizational performance. Those choices are informed by deeply rooted beliefs that form the two symbolic orders—ethos and world view. Sport management, therefore, seeks, in its own way, to harmonize a group of people's conception of the real with their conception of the appropriate way to behave in a particular environment. Hampden-Turner and Trompenaars (2000) and Trompenaars and Hampden-Turner (1997) have systematically interrogated the role of culture in solving management problems. They developed a sophisticated model and measuring instruments, which have been applied in the field of sport by Girginov, Papadimitriou, and D'Amico (2006) in a study on the cultural orientations of managers from seven countries. It was found that cultural predispositions push us to make particular choices of management approaches. Mintzberg, Simons, and Basu (2002) succinctly captured the difference between the Western model of management and other management practices. Mintzberg et al. proposed the notion of "engaging management" and compare it to heroic management taught in the West. They describe the former as "to manage is to bring out the energy that exists naturally within people. Managing thus means inspiring and engaging", and the latter as "to manage is to make decisions and allocate resources including 'human' resources. Managing means analyzing, often calculating" (p. 71). Mintzberg et al.'s (2002) argument challenges the logic of managerialism, which is premised on the management of finite resources in a fragmented policy area of sport.

Culture as Singular and Plural

The singular–plural aspect of culture raises important issues for sport management scholars and practitioners. Since sport management is a culturally conditioned activity it becomes identifiable in a number of different forms—from organizational, to sport-and-fan-specific cultures and artefacts. Those forms take shape and evolve largely underpinned by two interrelated processes of singularization and homogenization. We recognize an athlete, a club or a fan by the way they dress, behave and other identifiable clues they exhibit. Culture's inherent drive for discrimination makes them unique. At the same time, the need for sharing with fellow culture members and acting collectively to address common problems makes people demand the same sport service or equipment on a mass scale. This need, together with the striving for commodification of sport, is the basis for the homogenization of sporting cultures. As a result, the singularization drive urges sport managers to deal with issues, such as brand, organizational culture and diversity management and fan loyalty. In contrast, homogenization pushes managers to tackle wider issues of social inclusion, equality and how to make policy sense out of a universe of diverse cultures while preserving social control. For Clegg and Palmer (1996), the interplay between globalization and cultural fragmentation represents one of the fundamental paradoxes of management.

Culture as Dialectic of System and Practice

The dialectic of system and practice aspects of culture focuses on the process of systemic interaction. As Hofstede (1984, p. 82) observed, "management is a symbolic activity: that is, managers influence other persons through wielding symbols that have meaning for these persons and motivate them towards the desired action". The process of systemic interaction ensures that system and practice mutually reinforce each other. Adler (1983) and Hofstede (1984, 1996), among others, convincingly demonstrated that management theories and practices are culturally embedded; they stem from different epistemologies, as both make assumptions about the nature of human life, our relations with other people and attitudes to nature and time. It follows that various management theories and approaches, such as TQM, HCM, NPM, represent systems of meaning and practices. As Clegg and Palmer (1996, p. 3) put it, "management theory, as a body of knowledge, is thus a political discourse *par excellence*". The purpose of political discourse and the ideology which it represents is to incite people into action, sometimes in conformity and sometimes in opposition to leads by the state, business or voluntary sector organizations.

When advancing a particular theory, sport management scholars ought to be able to clearly position themselves to the rationale of their research. Building on Habermas' (1972) notion of knowledge-constitutive interests, which identified three basic motives in which any knowledge-seeking project is grounded, Alvesson (2002) proposed an approach to link the study of culture with organizations. He applied it to the investigation of organizational culture and demonstrated how similar studies can serve three different interests—technical (i.e. concerned with enhancing prediction and control), practical (i.e. to improve mutual understanding) and emancipatory (i.e. to expose and alleviate domination). Alvesson (2002, p. 12) maintained that management should not be seen "as a technocratic project where managerial agents engineer the minds of their subordinate objects, but as an interactive, interpretive enterprise". Thus, the social interaction between system and practice in sport carries social, political and economic consequences. From a research point of view this entails employing mixed methodologies to capture the system–practice dialectic in a mutually constructive but non-deterministic way. As Sewell (1999, p. 48) argued for the importance of recognizing the autonomy of culture, "culture is neither practical kind of practice nor practice that take place in a particular social location. It is, rather, the semiotic dimension of human social practice in general".

Culture as a System of Production

The above discussion leads to the sixth aspect of culture, which sees it as shaped by an underlying system of production. A society's system of production concerns the ownership of the means of production, the division of labour and the distribution of wealth. The core process related to this aspect is the socio-economic organization of sport. There are three basic models of organization of sport depending on whether the key mechanism for sport production and consumption is market- or state-led or a mixed economy. In a market-led model of sport provision, participation is a function of one's ability to pay, whereas in a state-led model it is a basic right.

The socio-economic organization of sport significantly affects sport management research agendas and curricula. It is no accident that in the market-led North American model of sport, research and teaching in the field has focused on marketing sport profitably, measuring organizational performance and global expansion of brands. In contrast, the European model of sport places greater emphasis on the role of non-profit sport organizations and their interaction with the state (Barros, Ibrahimo, & Szymansky, 2002). The study of different sport models and policies enables us both to see social relations in actions and to understand cultural systems; thus, it transcends the field of sport governance and management.

Culture as a Political Category

The political aspect of culture involves both the political recognition of multiculturalism as a policy issue and the existence of different political cultures. As Peters and Pierre (1998, p. 233) observed, "governance, as are all models of public service, is derived from the political culture within which it is embedded". What is more, as Shore and Wright (1997, p. 28) wrote, "culture is an increasingly important domain of governance through which modern states try to organize and control civil society". The political aspect also implies new forms of sport governance resulting from the constant negotiations of state–civil society boundaries. The recognition of cultural diversity in its various forms takes the analysis back to the key management function concerned with conferring order and social control. "Multiculturalism is substantive", wrote Hall (2000, p. 209) and explained that "it references the strategies and policies adopted to govern or manage the problems of diversity and multiplicity which multi-cultural societies throw up". For example, as gender, ethnic, disability and gay cultures become politically accepted, they automatically earn the right to equally participate in the decision-making process concerning the provision of sport. The core processes here involve designing systems of governance to guide and steer (politically and socially) collective decisions towards a satisfactory level of consensus amongst various parties concerned. Thus, the traditional role of bureaucratic hierarchies (e.g. state-led) and markets, as effective mechanisms for sport provision becomes problematic. Hall's (2000, p. 210) notion of commercial multiculturalism, which "assumes that if diversity of individuals from different communities is recognized in the market place, then the problem of cultural difference will be (dis)solved through private consumption, without any need for a redistribution of power and resources", helps to clarify the point. Instead, considering networks of autonomous agencies for ensuring successful collective action provides an alternative model of sport governance. As Rhodes (2007, p. 1252) argued, "we should focus on the social construction of policy networks through the ability of individuals to create meaning". Rhodes' point relates to the fifth aspect of culture as dialectic of system and practice. Thus, sport management scholars and practitioners need to go beyond the visible manifestations of culture and to engage with the substantive issues of power relations in the production and consumption of sport.

Sport Management Cultures: Conclusions

The discussion of the seven aspects of culture demonstrated that studying the culture–sport management nexus does matter. Culture and sport management share a fundamental function—both strive to create order and to avoid uncertainty. They, however, operate at two different but interconnected levels: while culture is more abstract and subtle, management is idiosyncratic and operational. Sport management, therefore, is always plural, as it represents a bounded world of beliefs and practices. Sport managers' beliefs, values and assumptions broadly constitute their "ethos", which is often interpreted as national culture or "collective programming of the mind". Managers' "world view" is representative of their practices, which follow a particular order grounded in their ethos. Similar to culture, sport management is dynamic and presents a unity of known ideas and practices taught at educational institutions and learned on the job in various environments. At the same time, sport managers constantly offer and test new cultural meanings in their efforts to affect people's and organizations' attitudes and behaviours. Sport managers, therefore, become mediators of meanings who greatly influence the socialization and acculturation of people in and through sport. A political recognition of culture has significant implications for the governance and management of sport and suggests that we need to reconsider many taken-for-granted concepts, such as "developed–underdeveloped", "strategic planning", "effectiveness", "human resource" and "control".

Culture's striving for singularization, however, should not lead us into the realm of cultural relativism in sport management. The challenge here is not to lose one's point of reference and to develop a cultural competency. We all carry the cultural imprints of our families, religions, gender, ethnicity and societal influences which make us who we are. There is no need to abandon our cultural make up and to pretend to be another person culturally. Rather, we need to develop our cultural sensitivity, which will enable us more easily to accommodate different cultural views and to build bridges between diverse individuals and organizations. As sport represents a vastly symbolic system, which has no equivalent in real life, sport managers need to be aware that the social and economic consequences of their actions may not always be positive but culturally insensitive and counterproductive.

What follows for the research, practice and teaching of sport management is that a culturally-informed approach to the field could bring substantial conceptual and practical benefits. The study of sport management can be used to understand various cultural systems, as even the most rigid legal contracts and regulations make little sense outside their cultural context. For example, the sport management curricula should not be afraid to offer space for courses on cultural history of society and sport, cross-cultural and comparative studies, or to critically interrogate the ideological nature of the management enterprise. This entails that the core management functions and processes (e.g. planning, organizing, controlling) cannot be taught and researched simply as neutral technical activities, but need to be seen in their relevant cultural context as well. Equally, serious consideration should be given to attempts at producing management tool kits and transfer of knowledge programmes designed to educate "the less-developed" or to promote "the best way of managing". This trend has been particularly evident in the growing number of international sport for development initiatives, the export of know-how in staging major sporting events and marketing campaigns, and sport legacy consultants. Assuming a position of power towards another culture is anti-cultural and inevitably leads to resistance and clashes. For example, often we do not think about the culture consequences when we teach a class on sponsorship or research its effectiveness. However, the reality is that in an attempt to ensure exclusivity and maximum return on investment, many sport managers actively reinforce a "provider–recipient" power relationship that privileges the sponsor by creating and controlling sporting spaces for branded consumption, often in sharp contrast with local cultural norms and traditions.

By focusing on culture, the sport management field of study changes. The researcher is no longer interested only in what makes people participate in sport, watch a game or how organizational structures are designed; rather, the sport management researcher is seeking to understand the underlying cultural processes that drive and facilitate people's and organizations' behaviours in sport. The emphasis shifts from exploring hierarchy as a property of sport organizations and a mode of governance to what does hierarchy actually mean in different locales, what cultural values and beliefs sustain it, and how those shape management practices. Sport management, therefore, could be seen both as a representation of the symbolic cultural system within which it operates and as a means of actively shaping this system. Sport managers thus become mediators of meaning, while sport organizations become institutions for socialization, acculturation and control.

Structure of the Special Issue

This volume brings together six contributions informed by a range of cultural perspectives and written by authors representing diverse cultures that touch on all seven aspects of the culture–management nexus. Each contribution offers original interpretations of culture and provides research and practical ideas—two contributions relate culture to sport policy, one to sport and fitness organizations, one to marketing and two to research and teaching. Furthermore, each study asserts the underlying message of this volume that culture does matter for sport management. Further to the introductory conceptual article on culture and the study of sport management by Vassil Girginov, first, Mahfoud Amara and Ian Henry address the issue of reconciliation of diverse cultures in sport policy. Multicultural policy is influencing Muslims' meaning systems around the issues and practices of sport and the role it can play in the process of social, cultural and intellectual re-positioning of Muslims in the West in general and in the UK in particular. The authors critically assess and reject the ethnocentrism of the twin opposing perspectives of Orientalism and Occidentalism and offer an approach that encompasses the dynamics associated with the Muslim presence in the West. Amara and Henry submit that policy development and management of provision in sport will be more effectively delivered in a context in which understanding of the world views of policy makers and targeted religious minorities is developed. Thus, this contribution highlights the systemic-practice and political aspects of culture.

Eric MacIntosh, Alison Doherty, and Matt Walker engage with the interpretation of culture at organizational level. The authors investigate whether there are certain commonly shared values by the not-for-profit and private fitness organizations in Canada. It is suggested that despite differences in the underlying philosophies of both sectors and small cross-sector variations, shared values do exist in the Canadian fitness industry that guide staff behaviour and organizational practice. This study is positioned within the normative aspect of culture. Hazel Maxwell and Tracy Taylor examine the development of a culture of trust between Muslim women and community sport organizations in Australia. This is achieved through an analysis of women's participation in sport and its role in developing social capital. It is demonstrated that the three different forms of social capital—bonding, bridging and linking—play an important role both for reaffirming original cultural values and predispositions, and cultural adaptations in the positions of the host and the newcomer. This study is an example of the *nomos* and innovative aspects of culture.

Artemisia Apostolopoulou, Dimitra Papadimitriou and Vasia Damtsiou employ a symbolic-interpretative perspective to investigate the cultural meanings and functions of Olympic consumption, using the case of the 2004 Athens Olympic Games. The study reveals that the consumption of Olympic-licensed products is not simply an exchange process, but was marked by highly symbolic cultural meanings embedded in the consumption and, as such, falls into the singular–plural aspect of culture. Finally, Steven Pope engages with the visible and indicative characteristics of culture, such as race, gender, equity, human rights, power relations and geography. He notes the methodological limitations of most of the sport management teaching and research as still grounded in a positivist Western ontology and proposes a culturally-informed interpretation through a reflective analysis of a new collection of sport management readings. Pope's analysis is located in the dialectic of system and practice aspect of culture.

Despite the variety of interpretations of the culture–sport management nexus offered by this collection, there is still a great deal of work to be done in understanding those links and their implications for researching, teaching and practising in the field.

Note

1. Ranked 2nd impact factor in management in 2009 by the Journal Citation Report—for those who insist on the importance of impact journals.

References

Adler, N. (1983). A typology of management studies involving culture. *Journal of International Business Studies*, *14*, 29–47.

Allison, M. (1982). Sport, culture and socialization. *International Review for the Sociology of Sport*, *17*(11), 11–37.

Alvesson, M. (2002). *Understanding organizational culture*. London: Sage.

Alvesson, M., & Sveningsson, S. (2008). *Changing organizational culture: cultural change work in progress*. London: Routledge.

Amis, J., & Silk, M. (2005). Promoting critical and innovative approaches to the study of sport management. *Journal of Sport Management*, *19*(4), 355–366.

Andrews, D. (2002). Coming to terms with cultural studies. *Journal of Sport & Social Issues*, *26*(1), 110–117.

Andrews, D., & Giardina, M. (2008). Sport without guarantees: toward a cultural studies that matters. *Cultural Studies Critical Methodologies*, *8*(4), 395–422.

Barley, S., Meyer, G., & Gash, D. (1988). Culture of culture: Academics, practitioners and the pragmatics of normative control. *Administrative Science Quarterly*, *33*(1), 24–60.

Barros, C., Ibrahimo, S., & Szymansky, S. (Eds.) (2002). *Transatlantic sport: The comparative economics of North American and European Sport*. Northampton: Edward Elgar Publishing.

Bartunek, J., Rynes, S., & Ireland, D. (2006). What makes management research interesting and why does it matter? *Academy of Management Journal*, *49*(1), 9–15.

Berger, P. (1973). *The social reality of religion*. Harmondsworth: Penguin Books.

Bloom, H., Calori, R., & de Woot, P. (1994). *Euromanagement: A new style for the global market*. London: Kogan Page.

Chadwick, S. (2009). From outside lane to inside track: sport management research in the twenty-first century. *Management Decision*, *47*(1), 191–203.

Chelladurai, P. (2001). *Managing organisations for sport and physical activity: A systems perspective*. Scottsdale, AZ: Hotcomb Hathaway.

Chen, M. (1995). *Asian management systems*. London: Routledge.

Choi, Y.S., & Scott, D.K. (2008). Assessing organizational culture using the competing values framework within American Triple-A baseball. *International Journal of Sport Management and Marketing*, *4*, 33–48.

Clarke, J., Gewirtz, S., & McLaughlin, E. (Eds.) (2000). *New managerialism, New welfare?* Maidenhead: Open University Press.

Clegg, S., & Palmer, G. (Eds.). (1996). *The politics of management knowledge*. London: Sage.

Colyer, S. (2000). Organisational culture in selected Western Australian sport organisations. *Journal of Sport Management*, *14*(4), 321–341.

Cunningham, G.B. (2007). *Diversity in sport organizations*. Scottsdale, AZ: Holcomb Hathaway.

Cunningham, G., & Fink, J. (2006). Diversity issues in sport and leisure. *Journal of Sport Management*, *20*(4), 455–465.

Donnelly, P. (1996). The local and the global: globalization in the sociology of sport. *Journal of Sport & Social Issues*, *20*(3), 239–257.

Dutton, J., & Dukerich, J. (1991). Keeping an eye on the mirror: Image and identity in organisational adaptation. *Academy of Management Journal*, *34*(3), 517–554.

Eagleton, T. (2000). *The idea of culture*. Oxford: Blackwell.

Flynn, N. (1997). *Public Sector Management*. Hemel Hempstead: Prentice-Hall/Harvester.

Geertz, C. (1973). *The interpretation of cultures: Selected essays*. New York: Basic Books.

Girginov, V., Papadimitriou, D., & D'Amico, R. (2006). Cross-cultural competence of sport managers. *European Sport Management Quarterly*, *6*(1), 35–66.

Groeschil, S., & Doherty, L. (2000). Conceptualising culture. *Cross Cultural Management—An International Journal*, *7*(4), 12–17.

Habermas, J. (1972). *Knowledge and human interests* (trans. J. Shapiro). London: Heinemann.

Hall, E.T. (1976). *Beyond culture*. New York: Anchor Press.

Hall, E.T., & Hall, M.R. (1990). *Understanding cultural differences*. Yarmouth, MA: Intercultural Press.

Hall, S. (2000). Conclusion: the multi-cultural question. In Hesse, B. (Ed.), *Un/settled multiculturalisms: Diasporas, entanglements, 'transruptions'* (pp. 209–240). London: Zed Books.

Hampden-Turner, C., & &Trompenaars, F. (1993). *The seven cultures of capitalism*. London: Piarkus.

Hampden-Turner, C., & Trompenaars, F. (2000). *Building cross-cultural competence*. London: Yale University Press.

Hofstede, G. (1980). *Culture consequences*. London: Sage.

Hofstede, G. (1984). Cultural dimensions in management and planning. *Asia Pacific Journal of Management, January*, 81–99.

Hofstede, G. (1993). Cultural constraints in management theories. *Academy of Management Executive*, *7*(1), 81–94.

Hofstede, G. (1996). An American in Paris: The influence of nationality on organization theories. *Organization Studies*, *17*(3), 525–537.

Hofstede, G., Neuijen, B., & Ohavy, D.D. (1990). Measuring organizational cultures: a qualitative and quantitative study across twenty cases. *Administrative Science Quarterly*, *35*, 286–316.

Holden, N. (2002). *Cross-cultural management: A knowledge management perspective*. London: Prentice Hall.

Hong, Y. (2009). A dynamic constructivist approach to culture. Moving from describing culture to explaining culture. In R. Wyer, C. Chiu, & Y. Hong (Eds.), *Understanding culture: Theory, research and application* (pp. 3–23). New York: Psychology Press.

Hughson, J. (2009). The making of sporting cultures: introduction. *Sport in Society*, *12*(1), 1–2.

Inkeles, A., & Levinson, D. (1969). National character: The study of module personality and socio-cultural systems. In Lindsay, G. & Aronson, E. (Eds.), *The handbook of social psychology* (2nd ed.) (pp. 418–506). Reading, Mass.: Addison-Wesley.

Jung, T., Scott, T., & Davies, H. (2009). Instruments for exploring organisational culture. *Public Administration Review, November/December*, 1087–1096.

Kluckhohn, F., & Strodtbeck, F. (1961). *Variations in value orientations*. Westport, Conn: Greenwood Press.

Kopytoff, I. (1986).*The cultural biography of things: Commoditization as process*. In A. Appadurai (Ed.), *The social life of things. Commodities in cultural perspective* (pp. 64–91). Cambridge: Cambridge University Press.

Kroeber, A.L. & Kluckhohn, C. (1952). *Culture: A critical review of concepts and definitions*. Cambridge, MA: Peabody Museum.

Lessem, R., & Neubauer, F. (1994). *European management systems*. London: McGraw-Hill.

Lewis, R.D. (1992). *Finland: Cultural Lone Wolf: Consequences in international business*. Helsinki: Richard Lewis Communications.

Linstead, S. (1997). The social anthropology of management. *British Journal of Management*, *8*, 85–98.

Maruyama, M. (1984). Alternative concepts of management: Insights from Asia and Africa. *Asia Pacific Journal of Management, January*, 100–111.

McGuire, D., O'Donnell, D., Garavan, T., Saha, S., & Murphy, J. (2002). The cultural boundedness of theory and practice in HRD? *Cross-Cultural Management: An International Journal*, *9*(2), 25–44.

Mintzberg, H., Simons, R., & Basu, K. (2002). Beyond selfishness. *MIT Sloan Management Review, Fall*, 67–74.

Morden, T. (1999). Models of national cultures—A management review. *Cross Cultural Management*, *5*(1), 19–44.

Mwaura, G., Sutton, J., & Roberts, D. (1998). Corporate and national culture—an irreconcilable dilemma for the hospitality manager? *International Journal of Contemporary Hospitality Management*, *10*(6), 221–220.

Peters, G., & Pierre, J. (1998). Governance without government? Rethinking public administration. *Journal of Public Administration Research and Theory*, *8*(2), 223–243.

Pitter, R., & Andrews, D. (1997). Serving America's underserved youth: reflections on sport and recreation in an emerging social problems industry. *Quest*, *49*(1), 85–99.

Pope, S., & Nauright, J. (Eds.) (2009). *The new sport management reader*. Morgantown: Fitness Information Technology.

Powell, M. (1995). Culture: intervention or solidarity. *Development in Practice*, *5*(3), 196–206.

Quarterman, J., Hwang, J., Han, K., Pitts, B., Jackson, T., & Ahn, T. (2010). A content analysis of the International Journal of Sport Management. Poster presented at the AAHPERD, Strength Through Partnership conference, 16–20 March.

Rhodes, A. (2007). Understanding governance: Then years on. *Organisation Studies*, *28*(8), 1243–1264.

Richman, B. (1977). Significance of culture variables. In T. Weinshall (Ed.), *Culture & management* (pp. 15–38). New York: Penguin Books.

Seagrave, S. (1995). *Lords of the Rim: The invisible empire of the overseas Chinese*. London: Bantam Press.

Sewell, W. (1999). The concept(s) of culture. In E. Bonnell, & L. Hunt (Eds.), *Beyond the cultural turn* (pp. 35–61). University of California Press.

Shore, C., & Wright, S. (1997). *Anthropology of policy*. London: Routledge.

Smith, A., & Shilbury, D. (2004). Mapping cultural dimensions in Australian sporting organizations. *Sport Management Review*, *7*, 133–165.

Smith, P., Peterson, M., & Wang, M. (1996). The manager as mediator of alternative meanings: A pilot study from China, the USA and UK. *Journal of International Business Studies*, *27*(1), 115–137.

Sport England (2002). *No limits Sport England's equity policy*. London: Sport England.

Stocking, G. (1966). Franz Boas and the culture concept in historical perspective. *American Anthropologist*, *68*, 867–882.

Todorova, M. (1997). *Imagining the Balkans*. Oxford: Oxford University Press.

Trompenaars, F., & Hampden-Turner, C. (1997). *Riding the waves of culture*. London: Nicholas Brealey Publishing.

Watson, T. (1994). *In search of management: Culture, chaos & control in managerial work*. London: Routledge.

Williams., R. (1989). Culture is ordinary. In A. Gray, & J. McGuigan (Eds.), *Studying culture: An introductory reader* (pp. 5–14). London: Edward Arnold.

Sport, Muslim Identities and Cultures in the UK, an Emerging Policy Issue: Case Studies of Leicester and Birmingham

MAHFOUD AMARA & IAN P. HENRY

School of Sport, Exercise and Health Sciences, Loughborough University, Loughborough, UK

ABSTRACT An understanding of diversity and its implications for policy is critical to those charged with delivering sporting services in culturally plural societies. This paper reports a research project which aimed to examine how, on the one hand, Muslims in two specific local contexts in the UK (Leicester in the East Midlands; Birmingham in the West Midlands) make sense of the relationship between their religious (Islamic) identities and sporting interests and, on the other, how local policy makers perceived and responded to the sporting needs of these Muslim communities. According to the 2001 census, Leicester and Birmingham represent, respectively, one of the most ethnically diverse areas in Britain and the domicile for one-third of the Muslim population in Britain. Interviews were undertaken with representatives of Muslim organizations, governmental and quasi-governmental sporting organizations, in both cities. Critical Discourse Analysis of interviewees' responses reveal pluralistic views on a range of issues such as: the "(un)suitability" of the environment/space provided for, or accessed by, Muslims to practise sport; funding; gender equity; equity and social inclusion agenda versus cultural and religious diversities; and a resistance (on the part of policy makers) to target provision at faith groups.

Introduction

The dominant line in Western literature on the emergence of modern sport in nineteenth-century Europe argues that it was associated with the advent of capitalism, industrialization, urbanization and the nation-state system. Thus, based on the idea of regulation, disciplining of the body, aestheticism, meritocracy, division of labour, bureaucratic organization and rational measurement of performance, modern sport, particularly in its competitive form, constructed its meaning and value system in opposition to "traditional" (magic-ritual/folkloric, "pre-modern") physical practices (Guttmann, 1978). Accordingly, the acceptance of modern sport practices has been seen as a sign of "assimilation" of (Western) modernist values and, thus, of the Western (universal) "civilizational" project. This is also true in relation to the debates on integration or socialization through sport in Europe, which apply modern sport as the norm and as a reflection of some core values of Western culture and civilization. Yet this linking of modern sport to Western secular and rational modernity has consigned those physical activities attached to religious belief to the domain of tradition and, thus, the non-engagement with (or resistance to) modern sport by Muslim minorities is seen by some as reflecting a lack of integration into European societies and cultures.

Within this context, the focus of the research reported in this paper is an evaluation of how Muslims in two specific local contexts, in the UK (Leicester in the East Midlands; Birmingham in the West Midlands) make sense of the relationship between their religious (Islamic) identities and sporting interests. Leicester in the East Midlands and Birmingham in the West Midlands have been selected because they represent, respectively, one of the most ethnically diverse areas in Britain (Leicester) and a domicile of one-third of the Muslim population in Britain (Birmingham) (Office for National Statisics, 2001b).

The concerns of this paper are particularly relevant to the principal issues addressed in this special issue in that a major focus is on the engagement of the local sports policy community with the cultural diversity of communities in contemporary multicultural societies and, specifically, with Muslim communities. The encounter of policy communities with pluricultural contexts is a neglected issue but one of growing importance for sport policy makers and service managers in increasingly ethnically diverse societies.

A principal aim of this study is to understand how the status of Muslim communities' existence as a minority in the West (in these two English cities), has affected the way that Muslims conceive their identity, their Islamic practices (*Shari'a* or ways of living) and their relationships with the West. Of particular interest was also how this influences Muslims' meaning systems around the uses and practices of sport and the role that it can play in the process of social, cultural and intellectual re-positioning of Muslims in the West in general and in the UK in particular. A further aim was to identify the roles of sport in the social cohesion agenda and in cross-cultural dialogue between Muslim communities and other communities in Leicester and Birmingham. To this end we explored perspectives of representatives of local authorities and national sport organizations on the state of affairs as regards Muslim participation in sport and their rationale for policy in respect of the financing and provision of sport activities for Muslim organizations in Leicester and Birmingham.

As regards the structure of this paper, the literature review which follows is divided into three main sections. The first explores the current debate around multicultural policy and the question of the Muslim population in Britain. This is followed by a discussion of the current literature on sport and the question of Muslim minorities in the West. The methodology section subsequently highlights the philosophical and methodological positions of the authors and the approach adopted to data gathering and analysis. This is followed by a brief overview of the demographic and socio-economic profiles of the Muslim communities in both cities. The subsequent discussion is devoted to the examination of examples of emerging themes from the critical discourse analysis of interview transcripts and policy documents relating to the nature of sporting engagement by Muslim communities and their organizations.

Multicultural Policy and the Question of the Muslim Population in Britain

The riot provoked by Salman Rushdie's novel *The Satanic Verses*, and the Bradford incidents in 2001, are considered to be a turning point in the discourse around the question of integration of the Muslim population in Britain. These events accelerated or at least amplified demands by Muslims for legislation which would take into account their specific religious and ethnic identities (e.g. state funding of Islamic schools; laws which protect the status of Islam as a faith; and political representation) outside the realm of the dominant (black versus white) race discourse. In other words they increased pressure from Muslim groups to gain the same legal recognition as other religions (Christianity, Judaism and Sikhism) and the same protection as Catholics in Northern Ireland as regards legislation against religious discrimination. According to Modood, Triandafyllidou, and Zapata-Barrero (2006, p. 42),

> ...what was striking was that when the public rage against Muslims was at its most intense, Muslims neither sought nor were offered any social solidarity by any non-white minority. ... it was inter faith forums rather than political black organizations that tried to create space where Muslims could state their case without being vilified. Political blackness ... was seen as irrelevant to an issue which many Muslims insisted was fundamental to defining the kind of "respect" or "civility" appropriate to a peaceful multicultural society, that is to say, to the political constitution of "difference" in Britain.

The adoption the Amsterdam Treaty in 1997 recognized formally for the first time a requirement of equity of treatment of individuals by virtue of religious affiliation or belief in the context of Article 13 of the Treaty on European Union. This article thus provided the basis for religious and faith groups to be formally recognized in the UK's adoption of the 1998 Human Rights Act. The British government agreed to fund seven Muslim

Schools (on the same basis enjoyed by approximately seven thousand Anglican and Catholic schools, some Methodist and 36 Jewish schools: Cowell, 2006; Modood et al., 2006). A further positive step toward monitoring the integration of minority religious groups, particularly Muslim communities, came in the modification of census questions in 2001 to include a question on religious affiliation, although this was not popular among secularists or among Muslims who did not want to be recognized on the basis of their religious identity in the public sphere. In 2004, Europe's first Islamic bank, the Islamic Bank of Britain, opened its first branch in Birmingham and Alp Mehmet was appointed as Britain's first Muslim Ambassador (to Iceland).

While a small number of Muslim organizations, such as the Federation of Student Islamic Societies established in 1962 and the UK Islamic Mission, had already been in existence since the early 1960s, this period also saw the appearance of a number of new organizations which found their identities in Islamic roots. The largest Muslim organization is the Muslim Council of Britain (MCB), which was officially established on 23 November 1997. The same year saw also the founding of The Muslim Association of Britain (MAB), the Federation of Islamic Organizations in Europe (FIOE) and the Mosques and Imams National Advisory Body (MINAB). Such activity led Kristiansen (2006, p. 21) to describe in an article in *Le Monde Diplomatique* the period after the election of New Labour as "a golden era of secured relations with British Muslims".

The Muslim community in Britain is not, of course, homogeneous in terms of its religiously related social practices or religiosity. The ethnically diverse nature of the Muslim population inevitably reflects a culturally diverse spectrum. In addition, in terms of theological interpretation/ traditions, British Muslim communities comprise a diverse range of traditions, in which four major tendencies are identifiable. The largest numbers of followers come from the Barelwi tradition, followed by Deobandi, then Jamaat-i Islam-inspired institutions and, finally, the Ahl-i-Hadith network. All of these are theological and interpretive trends imported into the UK with the arrival of the early South Asian communities in the 1960s and 1970s. The other minority groups are: *Shia'a* represented by Al-Khoei Foundation; and Sufi represented by the Sufi Muslim Council (with 102 affiliates) linked to the wider Naqshbandi Sufi movement.

The 9/11 and the 7/7 bombings represented a seminal moment for British Muslims. These events fostered an atmosphere of fear and brought to the surface the debate around multicultural policy in Britain. Trevor Phillips, Chairman for the Commission on Racial Equality, in April 2004 argued that Britain's policy of multiculturalism had gone too far and that there was a need to ensure that a core of British values remained intact (Baldwin & Rozenberg, 2004). The Home Secretary, Jack Straw, publicly opposed the wearing of the veil by Muslim constituents in particular contexts (Sturcke, 2006) and there was evidence, in some areas of government and the quasi-government sector, of a shift away from a dominantly multiculturalist agenda (which had come to be seen as encouraging "separateness") and towards interculturalism to promote common interests and a shared sense of belonging. This debate leads Mahajan (2007, p. 318) to identify uncomfortable questions emerging in British political debates around integration: "Will multiculturalism survive in this milieu? Will the emerging conflict reinforce the belief that immigrants/'outsiders' must integrate into the host society? Should a liberal democracy accommodate cultural diversity and make space for the expression of cultural differences?"

The significance of sport in debates around multiculturalism is regularly cited. Sardar (2006) for example points out that sport is often invoked to celebrate Multicultural Britain:

> There is no doubting the pride and hope many young British Pakistanis find in such England players as Sajid Mahmood, Kabir Ali and Owais Shah. Because of them, some will be supporting England; others will support both England and Pakistan with equal passion. This is the fruit of multiculturalism; and a product of manifold and hybrid identities.

In addition, the rhetoric of multiculturalism was very present in the bidding for the 2012 Olympic Games, to legitimate the British readiness to host the Olympic Games (proclaimed to be a wholly appropriate space for the expression/celebration of "cultural diversity" and "cultural exchange") and, by the same token, to de-legitimize "other" rival nations bidding for the Games and their policies toward ethnic minorities (Carrington & McDonald, 2008). This view, still evident on the London 2012 website (London 2012, 2009), was reiterated by the Chair of the London 2012 Organising Committee, Sebastian Coe, in his speech at the Opening ceremony of Islam Expo, one of the biggest Muslim cultural events in Europe, on 7 July 2006 (exactly one year after the London bombing).

> One of the imperative reasons why the IOC trusted London to take the project of organising the 2012 Olympic Games was the ability of the UK delegation to explain London's creative, diverse, and tolerant community. That the project of hosting the games was not just a project for six weeks but a project for the next fifty years (Coe, 2006, transcribed from digital recording by the authors).

To reflect the multiculturalism of the Games at the organizational level and as an important step to incorporation of Muslim communities in the organization of the Games, Coe announced at this event the appointment of Dr Muhammad Abdul Bari, the newly elected General Secretary of the Muslim Council of Britain, to the board of directors of the London Organising Committee of the Olympic Games and Paralympic Games (London Organising Committee of the Olympic Games, 2009).

The significance of sport and equity debates is illustrated by the measures adopted in the UK to promote equity generally in relation to access to sport (Table 1) and measures which relate rather more specifically to Muslim communities (Table 2).

Table 1. Examples of British legislation on equality and social inclusion/exclusion

Examples of government agencies/non-governmental organizations providing general services to ethnic minority/ immigrant communities	DCMS; Home Office (Immigration and Nationality Directorate, National Asylum Support Service, Race Equality Unit (REU)/Active Community Unit (ACU)/Community Cohesion Unit(CCU)/The Faith Communities Unit); Department for Children, Schools and Families; Cabinet Office (Social Exclusion Unit, Neighbourhood Renewal Unit); The Department of Health; The Department of the Environment; UK Sports Institute; UK Sports Council; Local government Association/The Improvement and Development Agency (IDeA)/Local authorities; Scottish Council for Minorities Rights; NI Council for Ethnic Minorities; The Central Council of Physical Recreation (CCPR); The British Refugee Council; Asylum Aid; Refugee Action
Examples of UK legislation on race equality, race relations, and diversity	Legislation covering race equality: the Race Relations Act (1976 and the Race Relations Amendment Act (2000). Gender equality: the Equal Pay Acts (1970 and 1980); Legislation on gender and sexuality: the Sex Discrimination Act (1975), Gender Reassignment Act (2003), Equality Act (Sexual Orientation) Regulations 2007. Legislation on disability: The Disability Discriminations Act (1995), The Disability Discrimination Act 2005. Legislation on religion and belief: Employment Equality (Religion or belief) Regulations (2003); Racial and Religious Hatred Act 2006, Equality Act (2006)
Examples of sport policies on community cohesion, diversity strategy, social inclusion.	*Achieving racial equality: A standard for sport* (Commission for Racial Equality, 2000). *Sporting future for all* (DCMS, 2000). *No limits: Sport England's equity policy* (Sport England, 2002). Sporting Equals' Community Development Strategy (2005–2008); *Equality and diversity strategy; The government's plan for sport* (UK Sport, 2001, 2002, 2003); *PAT 10 sport and social inclusion* (Cabinet Office, 2000).

Literature on Sport, Leisure and the Multiple Identities of Muslims in the West and in the UK

We should distinguish between three types of endeavour relating to sport and Muslim thought and, therefore, between three types of literature. These

Table 2. Examples of initiatives and reports addressing the sporting needs of Muslim communities in Britain

Organization	Initiative/report
The Open Society Institute	*Muslims in the UK: Policy for engaged citizenshi*" (2005). The report provided recommendations to the DCMS and the Department for Education and Skills to overcome the social exclusions of Muslim Youth. Some of these recommendations emphasized the centrality of sport.
Muslim Council of Britain	*Towards greater understanding: Meeting the needs of Muslim pupils in state schools* (2007). Comprises a number of recommendations in relation to the practice of sport and physical education in schools. *Islamophobia in football* (2009). MCB is a member of working group set up by the English Football Association to develop a clear, all-agency strategy in a bid to tackle anti-Semitism and Islamophobia in Football. The other members include: the Muslim Women Sports Foundation, Board of Deputies of British Jews, PFA, the Equality and Human Rights Commission, National Association of Muslim Police, FA Board Race and Equality Advisory Group, UK Football Policing Unit, the Football Foundation and the League Manager's Association.
The Muslim Women's Network (MWN)	*Public sector duty to promote equality on the grounds of religion* (2007). The report stated, under the subheading health issues for Muslim women in the UK, that: "One of the solutions for improving the health of Muslim women includes exercise".
Sport England	*New guidance in the design of sport facilities* (2005). Sport England introduced new guidance in the design of sport facilities based on the proportion of ethnic profile within the relevant facility catchment area, i.e. national, regional, community or neighbourhood, and also have regard to the potential for visitors and staff from ethnic groups. Some of these recommendations concern Muslim clients directly.
Show Racism the Red Card	In its campaign against racism in football, an educational DVD was produced, featuring the views of many top players and also young people discussing their views and experiences around Islamophobia

are: (a) material on sport in Islam, including the question of sport in Islam in the West; (b) sport in Muslim societies; and (c) Sport in Islamism. Each of these domains has its own ontological and/or epistemological debates, in other words, diverse ways of questioning the existence of, and knowing about, sport (Amara, 2008), though our focus here is predominantly on the first of these.

Among the relatively few empirical studies of sport and multiple Muslim identities in the West is that of Walseth (2006a, b). Data from Walseth's interviews illustrate how the sporting needs of young Muslim women who express an overt attachment to the values of the community might be different from those of a second group, which is more attached to the values of the host society, and that of a third, which takes both a religious and liberal attitude towards the traditions of the community and the values of mainstream Norwegian culture (see also Carrington, Chilvers, & Williams, 1987; De Knop & Theebom, 1995; Taylor & Toohey, 2002). Thus, Walseth's approach takes into account the hybrid position adopted by many Muslim Norwegian women (particularly from second and third generations of immigrants) between the values of the community and that of the host society. This is commonly interpreted in the literature as a position between "tradition" and "modernity" or, using Parry's (2004) typology in his work on sport and multiculturalism, between "illiberal" and "liberal" cultures. Walseth goes on to suggest that sports federations in Norway should apply different strategies of integration for different contexts.

The question of the clash between cultural views and Islamic views is raised by Zaman in her work on the perceptions of young Bangladeshi women in the UK with regard to the link between physical education and well-being. In her analysis, Zaman (1997: 61) suggests that "they (interviewees) believed Bangladeshi culture tended to disapprove of women doing sport". Carrington and McDonald (2008), in analysing the different discourses shaping policy making around sport and social policy in the UK, assert that the shift in the past was from a concern for social control toward managing racial inequalities, whereas in the contemporary context, the shift is from racial equality to human rights. It was in the 1980s that, in response to "race riots', anti-racist policies based on the concept of multiculturalism "were most vigorously pursued" as a substitute for an "assimilationist model of race relations" (Carrington & McDonald, 2008, p. 236). However, the authors, in referring to the work of Barker (1981) on new racism, Hess (2000) on fluid ethnicity versus static race and Gilroy (1987) on ethnic absolutism, express their reservations about the term multiculturalism.

Tariq Ramadan (2002, 2004) is well known for his attempt to develop an "alternative" or "extended" Muslim position which seeks to be both faithful to the fundamental tenets of Islam and consistent with contemporary reality of European life. Ramadan is one of the few Muslim scholars in Europe who addresses the question of sport and recreation among Muslim communities in the West, and he argues that there is a problem relating to Islamic thinking about sport and leisure:

> If there was a domain where we are finding difficulty to promote an alternative project, it is definitely that of leisure and recreation. If we were to study the activities offered here and there we would notice three major deficits: either everything, or almost all, is "forbidden"; or we perpetuate activities coming from "elsewhere" which are inadequate to our current context; or lastly, we propose activities which are mostly child-like, and sometimes childish, without considering the age of those (males and females) to whom these activities are offered. By looking at adolescents (of both sexes) as if they were perpetual children of eight or ten, we will end up pushing them to search, elsewhere, for what they think are fitting leisure activities for their age and expectations. ... We need to embark upon the universe of leisure by intelligent selection and ethical complement (Ramadan, 2002: 60–63, translated by the authors from the French).

There is a number of other recently published papers which address the question of Muslim youth identities, migrations and the pursuit of leisure in Western contexts. Stodolska and Livengood (2006) interviewed 24 Muslim immigrants from Jordan, Lebanon, Iraq and Egypt. They stress the relation between leisure, faith and family ties, "the effect of Islam and leisure behaviour manifests itself through the emphasis on strong family ties and on family oriented leisure among Muslims" (Stodolska & Livengood, 2006, p. 293). Silverstein, focusing on young immigrants in the UK and France argues that host (ex-colonial) societies, such as Britain and France, are witnessing the beginnings of "reverse colonization" characterized by the loss of control by the state over "immigrant bodies". In Britain the effects of this are being felt in the sports sector, particularly within cricket and soccer. The threat of a loss of control over immigrant bodies in Britain and of political Islam in France has led, Silverstein suggests, in the French case at least, to attempts by the state to "re-master immigrant bodily practices" through sport at youth level (Silverstein, 2002, p. 11).

Methodological Approach

It should be noted that the approach adopted in this study, at what might be described as a meta-level, is bi-directional. It rejects the twin opposing perspectives, which are mirror image forms of ethnocentrism: (a) Orientalism (Said, 1991), which tends to link "violence", "superstition" and "irrationality" to Islam as a revealed religion; and (b) Occidentalism, which builds its identity (Muslimness) exclusively in relation to the "other"; in the form of the "evil", "atheist", "imperialist" and "morally corrupt" West. In addition, we differentiate between modernity as a project for society, which may take different (local and global) forms, and modernity as a "dogma" displacing religious absolutism with an anti-traditional, anti-religious (anti-clerical) and scientific essentialism. Haddad (2001) stresses that the use of anti-Islamism for ideological, mediatized and mercantilist aims should be condemned. However, the same is also true for the exploitation of Islam for purely temporal and political interests. Our endeavour is thus neither to impose a Western-centric vision of Islam in

Europe (or what should be a "European Islam") nor an Islamic judgement (in the sense of *Usul ul-Fiqh*, Islamic jurisprudence) of what is permissible (*Halal*) or illicit (*Haram* in Islam), but to provide an approach which embraces and encompasses the dynamics associated with the Muslim presence in (and of) the West, as an alternative to "Occidentalist" versus "Orientalist" polar views.

The Muslim Population in the Cities of Birmingham and Leicester

Birmingham

There are 140,033 (14.3%) people resident in Birmingham who declared themselves to be Muslim (the average for England is 3.1%) in the 2001 census. Only 6 of the 354 English Local Authorities have a higher percentage of Muslims. However, with this total of 140,033, Birmingham has a greater number of Muslims than any other local authority area. Of Birmingham's Muslim population, 71.7% live in seven wards of the City. These wards are Sparkbrook (19,372), Bordesley Green (18,629), Washwood Heath (16,847), Springfield (13,461), Aston (12,381), Lozells & East Handsworth (10,853) and Nechells (8,822). 104,017 (10.6%) have a Pakistani background, while 20,837 (2.1%) are of Bangladeshi origin. The other Muslim minority communities living in Birmingham include: Albanians, Bosnians, Somalis, Kurds, Afghans and Iranians. In relation to geographical concentration, many of the city's ethnic minorities are found in the older, de-industrialized areas around the city centre, known as the "middle ring" (Office for National Statistics, 2001b) Birmingham's Muslim population is twice as large as the single highest concentration of Muslims outside of London. In April 2001, 9% of all 1.6 million British Muslims and 16 per cent of Britain's entire Pakistani population of 658,000 were found to be in the city of Birmingham.

In terms of religious affiliation, Birmingham's Pakistanis are Barelvi, Tablilghi, Deobandi, Hanifi or Jamaat-e-Islami, which are all variants of Sunni Islam (Robinson, 1988 in Abbas, 2005). Abbas (2005) explains that "one-in-seven of the city's inhabitants are Muslim and their unemployment rate is three times that of the overall city levels", and that they continue to be concentrated in some of the city's poorest wards. In addition he highlights other forms of disadvantage experienced by Muslims in the city.

In the Birmingham Sport and Physical Activity draft strategy (Birmingham City Council, 2003) it was argued that, according to national research, people from the Bangladeshi and Pakistani communities are one and a half times more likely to suffer ill health, and that diabetes amongst Pakistani and Bangladeshi people is over five times higher than in the general population. The same report indicates that research conducted through the City Living Panel showed that Black and Minority Ethnic (BME) communities participate less (in sport) than other groups in the City. For example, under one-third (30.5%) had used a leisure centre/pool/club/gym in the last twelve months, compared to 42.7% of the overall City population. The proportion drops to 12.7% for those of Bangladeshi heritage.

Leicester

The city selected as a second case study was Leicester, which is one of the most diverse communities in England, with a 30% BME population, the largest group being Asian/Asian British. This proportion is expected to rise to 50% by 2010, which will make Leicester the "first non-white majority city in Great Britain" (Omaar, 2008). It is a designated cluster area for dispersal of asylum seekers and an estimated 52 different languages are spoken in the city (Leicester City Council, 2004). Muslims represent 11.03% (30,885) of the total population of Leicester. Of these, 4,276 (1.53%) have a Pakistani background, while 1,926 (0.69%) are of Bangladeshi origin. More recent arrivals are from East Africa, Kosovo, Bosnia and Somali. The national rankings placed Leicester seventeenth in terms of the size of its Muslim population (third for Hindu and tenth for Sikh). An analysis of 2001 census data states that

> at 30,885, the Muslim community of Leicester was larger than had been expected, and was the only religious community to have increased significantly in size since an informal survey held in 1983, indeed it constitutes the 10th largest community in England and Wales (Bonney, 2003, p. 36).

Outside London, Leicester is Britain's most religiously diverse city (European Commission, 2008). Sardar (2008) describes Leicester as "a good example of a city where the Asian communities are well integrated".

In terms of the geographical concentration of the Muslim population, in Highfields, an inner-city area, 75% of inhabitants are Muslim. Leicester has 19 mosques and the most dominant Muslim organization (affiliated to the Muslim Council of Britain), active in education, social welfare, policing and interfaith work, is the Federation of Muslim Organizations (FMO), which refers to itself as "the voice of the city's 50,000 Muslims" (Kristiansen, 2006).

Method of Data Collection and Analysis

Fieldwork in this exploratory research study addressed two groups of organizations in relation to both cities. The first group was Muslim organizations (or organizations whose members were predominantly Muslim) using sport as part of their activities to target Muslim communities in Leicester and Birmingham. The second was public sector or quasi-governmental organizations serving the local populations in general, and Muslim populations in particular. In both cases interviews were undertaken and secondary sources reviewed. The secondary sources included annual reports, policy papers and statements, strategic plans, web pages and publicity materials.

Six interviews were conducted with each group, thus twelve in total. The interviews were semi-structured, lasted for between 40 minutes and two hours, were digitally recorded and transcribed and subsequently subjected to analysis (following a Critical Discourse Analysis approach) employing Nvivo software. Each of the interviewees was informed that anonymity would be respected in order to facilitate an open and frank exchange. In the case of representatives proposed by the Muslim organizations, all were male, while the members of the policy community interviewed included one female and one member of an ethnic minority group only. None of the interviewees from the policy community was a Muslim.

For the purposes of this research, access to six faith-based organizations in total was obtained in Birmingham and in Leicester: a sport organization; and two non-sport (educational-community services) organizations in Birmingham and three faith-based organizations in Leicester. Although they were all non-sport organizations, sport plays an important part in the strategies of each of these organizations. For the interviewees from these organizations, the interview questions were centred around the following issues:

- Islam as a frame of reference to reflect upon identity, who Muslims feel they are and what they want to be;
- perceptions on modern sport; sport and the construction of Muslims identities;
- the role of sport in cross- and inter-cultural dialogues within Muslim communities and between Muslims and non-Muslims in the UK; and
- obstacles and challenges for participation in sport, access to funding and sport facilities.

To complement the analysis of the perceptions and accounts of representatives from Muslim organizations, six interviews (and analysis of secondary material) were also undertaken with a number of public sector and quasi-governmental bodies in both cities, namely the local authority, the County Sport Partnership (CSP) in each of the cities and the regional office of Sport England for the East Midlands, and the West Midlands. As an exploratory research approach the focus was on unpacking the perspectives, the "assumptive worlds" (Wolman & Ford, 1996; Young, 1977) of the interviewees from the policy community (and those of authors of supplementary materials in these organizations) rather than on obtaining an "objective record" of policy initiatives. The perspectives of the interviewees, who had been selected on the basis of their strategic roles in policy within these bodies and the authors of the documentation from their organizations, was what was sought rather than an "objective" description of the projects themselves.

The idea behind this strategy for collecting data was to have insights into both "top-down" (policy actors) and "bottom-up" (local Muslim actors) approaches to make sense of the positions of Muslim participation in sport, and of provision of sport for Muslim communities in Leicester and Birmingham, as well as of the policies/programmes adopted to meet the specific needs of the Muslim population.

Critical Discourse Analysis (CDA) was employed as the principal method of analysis in order to grasp the pluralistic (hybrid) discourses of the interviewees from the Muslim organizations and the policy community relating to sport and Islam and related policy. Our rationale for applying discourse analysis was informed by our research position, which seeks to give to "others" (Muslim scholars, leaders, intellectuals, members of Muslim movements and associations) a voice to define their own concepts of sport without privileging one discourse over another. CDA is particularly appropriate in such contexts since it focuses on understanding discourse "in relation to social problems or structural variables such as race, gender, class, and power, and seeks to unmask ideologically permeated and often obscured structures of power, political control and dominance, as well as discriminatory inclusion and exclusion" (Wodak, De Cillia, Blüml, & Andraschko, 1989, p. 8).

This kind of discursive construction or "analytical intervention" is helpful in illustrating how Muslims construct their religious identities in relation to their religious practice, the institutionalization of their religion and as members of the national community as a result of their current situation (as minorities in a Western secular context, in the wake of 9/11 and 7/7). Specifically, the study also attempts to identify the action and strategies adopted in relation to modern sport in a Western milieu. In particular we ask whether the strategy is one of, in Akbar's (2007) terms, "accepting", "preserving" or "synthesising". According to Akbar (2007, p. 33),

> Islam attempts to differentiate its various approaches or worldviews, some of which overlap while some are in opposition. These approaches can best be summarised as "accepting", "preserving" and "synthesising" ... Hence Islam's response to the forces of globalisation also takes at least three distinct forms: mystics reach out to other faiths, traditionalists want to preserve the purity of Islam, and modernists attempt to synthesise society with other non-Muslim systems.

Finally, the analysis of the Muslim actors' accounts is juxtaposed with the "top-down" analysis which seeks to uncover aspects of the world view of policy actors and their understanding of policy approaches adopted and the ways in which, and extent to which, they perceive themselves and these policies as serving the needs of Muslim communities.

Examples of Emerging Discourses on Sport, Identity and Policy

(a) Selected Discourses among Representatives of Muslim Organizations in Leicester and Birmingham

The theological considerations around sporting practice and sport provision in Britain and the (religious) criteria for the selection and organization of sport activities were constructed in interviewees' responses around the general rules or *Shari'a* guidance and not necessarily following the specific interpretation of a particular scholar or a *Fetwa* body either in Europe (e.g. the European Council of *Fetwa*) or in other parts of the Muslim world. Some of the religious parameters cited involved the dress code (for males and females) in a public domain; general Islamic rules of *halal* and *haram* (e.g. alcohol and gambling); and code of conduct or *Muaamalate*, which regulates relations within the Muslim community and between the Muslim community and other communities, as well as in relation to the laws of the state.

Most of the organizations which participated in this study emphasized that Islam as a tradition and a bodily culture is rich enough to make sense of sport. What has changed since the early history of Islam is the type of sport practices being undertaken. The emphasis, as explained by a representative of an organization in Leicester, has been to encourage values, such as team spirit and sense of "brotherhood" (*sic*), and to endorse a healthy lifestyle among Muslims. The selection of sport activities to promote these values tends to be dictated by the available sport facilities and not necessarily by a literal interpretation of the *Sunna* (the Prophet's tradition)

> there are some organizations in Leicester that have gone down the very traditional route and have introduced Archery clubs, because it was Sunna (tradition) of the Rasul (PBUH). That's a great practice. If we had the space and there was a demand we would encourage that within this facility here as well. We haven't taken a strict literal interpretation of what the Prophet was doing when he encouraged horse riding and encouraged archery. Because both of those are means of keeping men (*sic*) strong. Keeping them active. So we've tried to encourage those sports that a) we can accommodate; and b) those sports that encourage team playing, encourage sense of community, encourage sense of brotherhood (*sic*) and c) where obviously the individuals can get some benefits from doing their physical exercise (interviewee from Leicester, 11 June 2008).

Clearly, in this quote (and many others), the focus on sport for and by Muslims is on male Muslims, even though riding and archery are sports for which there is a widely recognized Koranic authority for women's participation. This is a point to which we shall return.

For some, the mosque as a religious and extensively a social institution can provide the ideal environment for Muslims to practice sport, as well as for non-Muslims (as long as they respected or adhered to the Islamic values which organize the social relations in the mosque).

> Elders were very quick to realize that just to provide religious facilities and the core religious events: speeches, seminars and lectures, won't be sufficient to encourage young Muslims to feel that they were actually involved in Muslim activities and actively part of the Mosque. *We had experienced in other parts of Leicester young Asians Muslims who wanted to get involved in sport activities but the only facilities that were available to them were mixed facilities with other ethnic (*sic*) groups. And as a result they were introduced to elements that were not considered Islamic i.e. drugs, mixing with the opposite sex and so on. That kind of environment wasn't really conducive to the Muslim environment we want to develop.* It was clear that we wanted to have a sporting environment within the bound of the Mosque, within the Mosque complex, where young people and old people could

come and enjoy sport in an Islamic environment. In a single sex environment without any influences that are not Islamic. The benefit of that was obviously on a personal basis they manage to get the physical exercise they desired, but also ensured that they formed a relationship with the Mosque. Traditionally the sporting facilities were provided around prayer times *so they'll be coming in our Mosque for prayers and get involved in sporting activities. It allowed us to really build a sense of community, especially amongst young Muslims* (interviewee from Leicester, 11 June 2008, emphasis added).

The other major discourses that emerged from interviewees' responses include the traditional discourse of "Us" and "Them" in identity formation. This was discussed by interviewees in relation to the West and Western culture. This was apparent in the discourse relating to the status of faith organizations in a secular milieu, or with regards to the "tactics" that Westerners or those representing Western interests (largely local authorities, Sport England, the church and schools) adopted in providing justification for not supporting Muslim organizations financially (at least back in the late 1980s). "Us" and "Them" discourse was also evident *within* the Muslim community, particularly in relation to the debate on majority and minority interests (defined more in ethnic rather than in theological terms, i.e. Somali rather than Pakistani Muslims as opposed to *Sh'iaa* versus *Sunna* interests).

Furthermore, interviewees' responses emphasized the question of prejudices relating to Muslim communities in the UK, particularly after the 9/11 and 7/7 terrorist attacks. This is reflected in the following responses:

it appears that the whole Muslim community is being put in the dock and made answerable for the criminal activities of a tiny, tiny number of people. All these pressures that are on us have created an atmosphere of fear among the Muslim community. It is a community that feels under siege. They have got a siege mentality in their mind. To bring up their confidence in themselves we need the outside forces to understand when they are looking into the Muslim community ... what is it they want to do. The majority are law abiding citizens. In fact Islam is a law—*Shari'a* based faith, and within this *Shari'a* faith base our love for justice, law and order is very strong ... *I think there is need for a more aggressive marketing policy to encourage talents from these communities into main stream sports.* Many times when we have those events I do invite people like FIFA to come down for the football ground to see some young talents ... to see whether they can identify that there are potentials within our community. But it means that we have to do the step forward to try to encourage them to recognise the Muslim community. No body come to us and say there is under representation of your community, what can we do to help? So barriers still exist (interviewee from Leicester, 27 May 2008: emphasis added).

Note the curious shift (which might be interpreted as an East–West shift) from a religious set of concerns in the early part of the quote, to those emphasizing marketing and the development of sporting talent.

Some interviewees expressed resentment at what they perceived as uneven treatment of different faith communities.

...since 9/11 everybody is talking about targeting faith communities ... asking faith communities to talk to each other ... but it is a nonsense (nothing is happening in reality). They are not thinking seriously about the subject ... The Muslim community is not

> receiving any money ... the local authority did not put any penny here (i.e. in the building of the Central Mosque). They give churches more money. Every Church (in the area) has been supported by the central government, but not mosques. These have all been built by the community (interviewee from Birmingham, 4 July 2008).

In relation to the gender issue, women's participation in sport was treated by the male interviewees as a theological-legal question. The non-mixing of genders is a core issue in the interviewees' responses in differentiating between the needs of Muslims and non-Muslims in relation to sport provision and in shaping the meaning of the "(un)suitability" of the environment/space provided for, or accessed by, Muslims to practice sport. However, the prejudice previously highlighted about Muslim communities in general was also formulated in relation to preconceptions that local authorities and Sport England have about the exclusion of women within the Muslim community and the rigidity that Islam may present with regards gender mixing.

> The greatest obstacle I think ... is the issue of religious sensitivities. *To fully understand how, for example, the issue of gender division can be brought.* We must not look at gender as an obstacle but we have to try and to find a way around it, which will meet the needs of that community. It is when we do not look at it as a problem but as a challenge ... how we can find answers to it is the way forward. We are at the moment in a culture where we seem to be critical of the Other ... *they will say that we don't want to participate with us. Rather than saying they are different we are different ... we are all different. Thus, how we can meet somewhere, where we can mutually respect each other. That is the challenge out there. We need to create that culture* (interviewee from Leicester, 16 May 2008, emphasis added).

To summarize this brief set of illustrations of the "bottom-up" perspectives, a shared aspect which links the emerging discourses together is the discursive strategy of "positioning" (Davies & Harré, 2006), as a product of both interaction with "the Other" and reflexive self-evaluation. These processes reflect Akbar Ahmad's (2007) categorization of Islam's responses to the forces of globalization, which he characterizes as being "accepting", "preserving" or "synthesizing". The interviewees exhibit a number of aspects with regards to the nature and function of sport.

- Acceptance of Western culture: accepting sport as a non-political domain, a universal culture or language, and as an element of the rich Islamic tradition and history.
- Preserving Islamic cultural heritage: regarding *Shari'a* as a dominant interpretative discourse in interpreting the meaning and the space (environment) where the practice of sport should take place. The practice/and access to sport in the vicinity of the mosque becomes a means of strengthening the relationship of the youth with their religion and thus preserving them from the negative elements of British society (e.g. drugs, crimes) as well as from extremism. Moreover, there is an avoidance of those forms of the equal opportunities debate which are seen as not in favour of preserving the purity of Islam.

- Synthesizing Muslim and non-Muslim traditions: integration of British values of active citizenship, inter-faith dialogue, community cohesion and marketing strategies in attracting funds; as well as women's rights, or at least their right to accommodate their sport practice to their faith (rather than in relation to equal representation within the organization).

(b) Selected Discourses among Representatives of Governmental and Quasi-governmental Sporting Organizations in Leicester and Birmingham

For the purposes of space we focus here on two elements of the discourses of members of the policy community: religious identity and the adoption of faith groups as policy targets; and gender as "*the*" problem of Muslim sports participation.

As we noted earlier, the signing of the Treaty of Amsterdam in 1997 was a turning point in defining discrimination on the basis of religious difference as contrary to the basic Articles of European Union. This was followed in the UK and elsewhere by adoption of human rights legislation and the adoption of related changes in strategy documents concerning equity goals to reflect this view.

As one might expect, equity issues had been clearly acknowledged as a policy focus in both the local authorities and County Sports Partnerships and at the regional and national level by Sport England. However, in all three contexts the descriptions of this formal acknowledgement placed less emphasis on defining disadvantaged groups by virtue of their religious identity, rather focusing on ethnicity or spatial concentration in disadvantaged areas, to frame equity policy for sport. Sport England, for example, in the definition of its equity policy specifically acknowledged "religious belief" as a dimension by which inequity is to be addressed: "Sports equity is about changing the culture and structure of sport to ensure that it becomes equally accessible to all members of society whatever their age, ability, gender, race, ethnicity, sexual orientation, *religious beliefs* or socio-economic status" (Sport England, 2002, p. 3; emphasis added).

Similarly, in the introduction to an updating of the equity policy, with the replacement of the Race Equality Standard by the more generic Equality Standard outlined in Sport England (2007, p. 7), clear reference is made to promoting diversity and equality of opportunity in ways that are sensitive to religion or belief.

> We aim positively to promote diversity and equality of opportunity in Sport. We can only achieve this if we are sensitive to differences of gender, race, disability, sexual orientation, transgender, age and *religion or belief* and free of discrimination as an employer and partner. We also believe we make better decisions if we are truly representative of the community we serve (emphasis added).

However, when the specifics of what is *required* by the legislation are identified there is effectively no mention of religious difference as being a dimension to which policy actions will be addressed. The document simply outlines "race specific duties", and is silent on how these duties might entail engagement with faith groups.

Against this background gauged from the policy documentation, where there is little other than a generic commitment to the forms of inequity experienced by religious or faith groups, the interviews provided interesting commentaries on related issues. At regional level one of the officers interviewed held a policy brief for equity policy beyond the region. He pointed to profiling work with the Active People Survey (Sport England, 2009) and to engagement with faith groups in discussion or dialogue and *de facto* engagement with groups which drew their membership predominantly from Muslim communities. However, with the exception of three schemes for Muslim women, he did not identify specific projects which overtly addressed religious groups' specific needs.

> My work has incorporated dialogue with the West Midlands Faith Forum for example where that's been a discussion in relation to the impact or the contribution that religious communities make to the kind of wider sports agenda around community cohesion but also the impact in terms of participation through participation in particular groups and there are ... I am conscious there a number of specific organizations working with faith communities around. Some of the Sisters Games is a good example in the Birmingham area where there's work with Muslim women around sporting opportunities that are culturally appropriate and opportunities for them to participate. In terms of the work ... (interviewee, West Midland Office of Sport England, 17 July 2008).

One should note here the emphasis on how faith communities might contribute to "Sport England's agenda" rather than a focus on meeting the needs of the groups *per se*. These ends are not necessarily incompatible but the rationale, even for this limited engagement, is on the usefulness of targeting religious groups to meet other governmental goals. Furthermore, despite this specific example of a group which was defined in terms of the religious affiliation of their members (see the Sisters' Games website which is located within the pages of Ummah.com – Muslim Forum; Sisters Games, 2009), the interviewee suggested that this was an exception to what was generally evident in the Birmingham context.

Interviewees from the East Midlands Regional Sport England Office were even more cautious about whether religious affiliation should be used as a means for defining target groups. In terms of identifying religious affiliation at the regional level they observed little effort made to even monitor the activities of faith groups. Indeed, the defining characteristics of sporting disadvantage are seen as being spatial (defining neighbourhoods as the locus of policy focus on the basis of spatial indicators of the concentration of disadvantage) and thus spatially-based responses simply dealing with the symptoms of disadvantage (its spatial concentration) rather than its causes:

> I suppose one of the big drivers for us was the Policy Action Team 10 report which talked about the role of sport and arts in terms of regeneration and the big policy shift at the time was around ... the Index of Multiple Deprivation and that's where over the last 7 years

> there has been all sorts of iterations but IMD has been pretty much a constant source of focus for us and again that takes you down to community areas rather than necessarily the communities they're in (interviewee, East Midland Office of Sport England, 19 July 2008).

At the local level of the CSP and local authority, a similar reticence to focus on religion was evident. In Birmingham the city's Race Equality Scheme 2007–2010 explicitly identified religious or faith groups as a subsidiary issue in race and equality: "The Equality and Diversity Division of the City Council was formed in 2004 with the aim of developing a more holistic approach to tackling inequalities based on faith, race, gender, sexuality, age and disability" (Birmingham City Council, 2007, p. 3).

And monitoring of faith groups in relation to disadvantage was required of those responsible for equity policy in sport in the City Council and CSP, which was seen as problematic if only because of the cultural complexity of the target populations for equity policy:

> historically our attention has been focused on gender, BME, disability and more recently have faith, sexuality and age being considered as priorities for us as a city. So the priorities have previously just been around maybe three focused areas, but it's now been extended because of legislative changes. ... we could certainly improve with our data collection linked to faith, because at this moment in time we don't particularly ask about faith, about users, so we don't really know who our users are in terms of faith, or should we say, we're inconsistent with this because sometimes we ask, sometimes we don't, ... so I would hope in the future we'd in a better position to be able to look at our profiles linked to faith and then be able to plan to how we need to deal or respond to issues like that (interviewee Birmingham City Council and CSP, 7 May 2009).

The situation in Birmingham was thus described as one of sporadic rather than systematic monitoring of differences by religious groupings, and limited intervention along faith group lines. Notwithstanding, there were two schemes which were cited by the Birmingham CSP interviewee as examples of targeting groups on the basis of religious identity. One was "The Aston Ward proposal: Young people, Muslims and community cohesion" (Birmingham City Council, 2008). This project, which was described as a direct product of security concerns, sought to link directly with Muslim youth in Aston, a ward with a 48% Muslim population, and with religious schools. It proposed a

> Three pronged approach looking to tackle (through sports) the problems related to community cohesion, disaffected young people in Aston and the engagement of the Madressas. ... Given that every Muslim child (under 12 with very few exceptions) will be attending a Madressa (normally for 2/2.5 hours in the evening between 16.00 and 19.30 (Madressa count in Aston—at least 12 officials [*sic*], with maybe at least as many unofficial ones). To target these young Muslims we will look to create links with all these Madressas, with a view to integrate/engage them into sporting activities of Aston Sports Club. Benefits to include: engagement of Muslims at an early age; engagement with Madressas with a view to integrate them into extended schools/ supplementary schools networks; healthy/sporting activities (Birmingham City Council, 2008, p. 1).

The second project, which was mentioned by a local authority interviewee (and was also identified by the Sport England regional representative), was the Saheli Women's Project. This group, though serving an almost wholly Muslim female population, had chosen to identify itself simply as a women's organization without a religious connotation to its membership or aims.

The perception of our interviewees in the Leicester context painted a broadly similar picture. Leicester had had the benefit of a funded Sport England scheme which had supported the Leicester Race Equality in Sport Project. However, this project was described as having operated without a focus on faith groups *per se*. Although it had sought on occasion to work through religious leaders, inter-group tensions were evident. However, since the project had ended in 2006, little progress was reported in trying to engage religious, particularly Muslim, groups. The establishment of Local Sports Alliances (LSA) is a national initiative intended to promote the engaging of local groups in local decision making about sport but one of the problems facing Leicester was that it had adopted a single city-wide LSA which was too big to promote engagement at the local level.

> So in that sense we've tried to work to develop the LSA, but we've had dozens of meetings now . . . and predominantly the people, the community, the people that we're able to get, apart from a few of the earlier meetings, . . . it's been white middle class, often males . . . So we're not getting those people from those communities representing their voices there (interviewee, Leicester-Shire & Rutland CSP, 16 September 2009).

One project mentioned by interviewees involved sporting matches between Muslim, Christian and Jewish clerics in the city, though this was initiated by the clerics themselves rather than being a project derived from the city or the CSP.

Although, as we have noted, the members of the policy community who were interviewed referred only rarely to the sporting and leisure needs of religious groups, the one area which attracted regular comment and attention was that of Muslim women. In essence raising the "problem" of Muslim sporting needs was often simply reduced to the issue of how to deal with the position of women in Muslim communities and how to go about making separate forms of provision. For example, the Sport England West Midlands regional officer identified three female organizations, two of which, the Muslim Women's Sports Foundation and the Sisters' Games, were explicitly focused on meeting the needs of Muslim women, while the other, the Saheli Women's Group, which *de facto* served local Muslim women and girls, adopted a more neutral approach to the market it served. In an interview featured on a promotional DVD, for example, one of its members describes the organization as serving the needs of "women and girls from any background, not just Muslim girls" (Saheli Women's Group, 2006). Two of these groups were also cited by CSP and City Council interviewees. The implication of these differing strategies is that the implicit definition of we/us and they/"the other" promotes a reaction in terms of who "the other" is for the women engaged in these groups, and for whom these women will themselves constitute "the other".

The approach of the Birmingham CSP was described in the following terms:

> In terms of the work of the County Sports Partnership . . . they've certainly been in discussion around a more kind of cultural brokerage approach, that is actually around appropriate provision for local neighbourhoods and certainly looked in terms of a neighbourhood model and certainly Birmingham for its action partnership in some of their sort of publications and national dialogue have tried to encourage an approach that's based around the identity of Muslim communities as people within the community rather than specifically highlighting Muslim faith as a kind of target group (interviewee, West Midland Office of Sport England, 17 July 2008).

This description emphasizes the notion of *brokerage*, with the CSP acting as a link between groups rather than accepting groups as part of the greater common whole, in other words reflecting the diversity of faith groups and associated religiosities. One way of dealing with some Muslim women's sporting needs is to refer to them as part of the sporting needs of a sub-set of women, those for whom participation is preferable or only possible in an all-female environment. However, while the need for most Muslim women for separate single-sex provision was recognized as a religious matter, and lack of women's participation was therefore seen as a bi-product of religious norms, men's low levels of participation was much more likely to be explained by factors associated with the spatial concentration of social deprivation.

Separate provision for the sexes, however, implied a cost in terms, for example, of staffing arrangements and practical rather than ideological issues were cited as reasons for not providing such services. There were, however, examples cited of separate provision having been made but with a lack of care in implementation, which may have been a reflection of a lack of appreciation of the requirements of, or empathy for, such an approach even though these were not new initiatives. Indeed, the political acceptability of this policy was not always clear cut and could provoke resentment among some:

> There are areas where women's specific provision, not actually in Birmingham, but women's specific provision particularly mindful of the needs of Muslim women around sort of dress code and single sex participation has created local kind of flashpoints, . . . response back from the British National Party kind of representatives . . . there's been some kind of hot issues if you like although less so in Birmingham than in other areas that I'm aware of (interviewee, West Midland Office of Sport England, 7 May 2009).

Conclusions

A major premise of this paper is that policy development and management of provision in sport will be more effectively delivered in a context in which understanding of the world views of policy makers and targeted religious minorities is developed. A range of issues have emerged from our exploratory research on the questions of sport practice among, and sport policy for, Muslim communities and these may be summarized as follows.

The debate on multiculturalism in Europe, and in the West in general, is today faced with a new challenge, which is to find a mechanism to reconcile Western culture and the Western history of modernity with so-called "non-Western" and ethnically more diverse cultures. Within this context there is a growing recognition of the specificity of Islam as a religion in the UK. New questions are thus being raised in relation to the practice of sport in the West. Demands are being made by Muslim organizations and Islamic faith centres (i.e. Mosques)—in the name of democracy, citizenship and rights to cultural and religious difference—to accommodate sporting practices to the specifics of Islamic religious practice, and for funding to build sports facilities and/or organize sport activities in suitable (e.g. gender-segregated) environments for males and females.

Despite the increased interest (within the public and voluntary sectors) in sport and Islamic faith as an emerging policy issue in the UK, multiculturalism in practice, particularly when it comes to dealing with the specific religious needs of Muslim communities, is constrained by other rhetorics, such as that of social inclusion and the ideology of Western liberalism. Hence, demands made by Muslim organizations for funding or for access to sports facilities, or to adapt sports practices to Islamic beliefs, are perceived as an obstacle to cross-cultural encounters and social integration. In the light of this difficulty, negotiation and re-appropriation of the space where sport practice by Muslim organizations should take place, and the redefinition of the central role of the Mosque as a place of worship but also a community centre offering diverse educational, cultural and even sporting activities are ingredients of the dynamics in identity formation within Muslim communities in the UK.

Although recent changes in legislation have resulted in some public bodies formally acknowledging religious and faith communities as appropriate targets for sport equity policy, interviewees reported a lack of practical action. An area of exception is that of (some) provision of women-only sessions in public facilities. However, for some in the policy community, the issue of provision for Muslim women appeared to be perceived as "the" (only) issue in relation to provision for Muslim communities. This policy was perceived as an issue relating to increasing participation rather than necessarily an issue in regard to (Western liberal norms of) emancipation *per se*. This issue is not well communicated by Muslim organizations, in part because of the relative lack of female representation among representatives in the Muslim organizations on which this study focused.

Policy goals on the part of the sport policy professionals for Muslim communities tended to be expressed in terms relating to the broader agenda of "sport (and health) for all", increased participation and enhanced access to existing provision, and community cohesion. This might be interpreted as an assimilationist approach concerned with getting Muslim groups to reach

British norms of participation, rather than identifying these communities' expression of their own needs.

Finally, we would argue that these tentative conclusions constitute elements which can contribute to the development of an intercultural understanding of the nature and roles of Muslim communities in contemporary Western/UK society. Such a task in the current climate is both relevant and important. As a consequence, our conclusions contain insights which, we would argue, are of direct relevance for policy in the field of sport and other social domains.

Acknowledgements

The authors would like to thank first the British Academy for financially supporting this study. Thanks also to representatives of Muslim organizations in Leicester and Birmingham, as well as representatives of local authorities and sport organizations in both regions for sharing their experiences and their views around the focus of this study.

References

Abbas, T. (2005). *Muslims in Birmingham.* UK Background Paper for COMPAS, University Of Oxford.

Akbar, A. (2007). *Journey into Islam, The crisis of globalisation.* Washington D.C.: Brookings Institution Press.

Amara, M. (2008). An introduction to the study of sport in the Muslim world. In B. Houlihan (Ed.), *Sport and Society: A student introduction* (2nd ed.) (pp. 532–553). London: Sage.

Baldwin, T., & Rozenberg, G. (2004, April 3). Britain'must scrap multiculturalism'. *The Times Online.* Retrieved November 1, 2008, from http://www.timesonline.co.uk/tol/news/uk/article1055221.ece.

Barker, M. (1981). *The new racism.* London: Junction Books.

Birmingham City Council. (2003). *Birmingham sports and physical activity draft strategy: Executive summary.* Birmingham: Birmingham City Council.

Birmingham City Council. (2007). *Race Equality Scheme 2007–2010.* Birmingham: Birmingham City Council.

Birmingham City Council. (2008). "The Aston Ward proposal: Young people, Muslims and community cohesion". Birmingham: Birmingham City Council, unpublished policy proposal.

Bonney, R. (2003). *Understanding and celebrating Religious Diversity. The growth of diversity in Leicester's places of worship since 1970s.* Retrieved October 10, 2008, from http://www.le.ac.uk/pluralism/Religious%20Buildings%20Introduction.pdf.

Cabinet Office. (2000) *PAT 10 Sport and social Inclusion.* London: Cabinet Office.

Carrington, B., Chilvers, T., & Williams, T. (1987). Gender, leisure and sport: a case-study of young people of South Asian descent. *Leisure Studies, 6,* 265–279.

Carrington, B., & McDonald, I. (2008). The politics of 'race' and sports policy in United Kingdom. In B. Houlihan (Ed.), *Sport and society, A student introduction* (pp. 230–254). London: Sage.

Coe, S. (2006). Inaugural speech, the opening ceremony of Islam Expo, 7 July.

Commission for Racial Equality (2000). *Achieving racial equality: A standard for sport.* London: The Stationery Office.

Cowell, A. (2006, October 15). Islamic schools at heart of British debate on integration. *International Herald Tribune.* Retrieved November 20, 2008, from http://www.iht.com/articles/2006/10/15/news/brits.php?page=1.

Davies, B., & Harré, D. (2006). Positioning: The discursive production of selves. In M. Wetherell, S. Taylor, & S. Yates (Eds.). *Discourse theory and practice: A reader.* (pp. 261–271). London: Sage.

DCMS (2000). *Sporting future for all.* London: DCMS.

De Knop, P., & Theebom, M. (1995). Sport and ethnic minority youth. *Journal of Comparative Physical Education and Sport, 17*, 12–13.

European Commission. (2008). *European year for intercultural dialogue: National strategy for the UK.* Retrieved January 25, 2009, from http://ec.europa.eu/culture/archive/dialogue/pdf_word/strategy_uk.doc.

Gilroy, P. (1987). *'There ain't no black in the Union Jack': The cultural politics of race and nation.* London: Hutchinson.

Guttmann, A. (1978). *From ritual to record. The nature of modern sports.* New York: Columbia University Press.

Haddad, M. (2001). *L'Islam est-il rebelle à la libre critique?* Paris: Panoramiques, Corlet et Marianne.

Hess, B. (Ed.) (2000). *Un/settled musliticulturalisms: Diaspora, etranglements, transruptions.* London: Zed Press.

Kristiansen, W. (2006, November 2). A visible statement of separation and difference: Britain's multiculturalism falters. *Le Monde Diplomatique.* Retrieved November 10, 2006, from http://mondediplo.com/2006/11/02ukmuslims.

Leicester City Council. (2004). *Supporting People Programme, Inspection report, June.* Retrieved November 10, 2009, from www.justice.gov.uk/inspectorates/hmi.. ./leicester_june1-rps.pdf.

London Organising Committee of the Olympic Games. (2009). The London 2012 Olympic and Paralympic Games. Retrieved November 1, 2009, from http://www.london2012.com/.

Mahajan, G. (2007). Multiculturalism in the age of terror: Confronting the challenges. *Political Studies Review, 5*, 317–336.

Modood, T., Triandafyllidou, A., & Zapata-Barrero, R. (2006). *Multiculturalism, Muslims and citizenship.* London: Routledge.

Muslim Council of Britain. (2007). *Towards greater understanding: Meeting the needs of Muslim pupils in state schools.* London: Muslim Council of Britain.

Muslim Council of Britain. (2009). *Islamophobia in football.* London: Muslim Council of Britain.

Muslim Women's Network (2007) *Public sector duty to promote equality on the grounds of religion.* London: Muslim Women's Network.

Office for National Statistics. (2001a). *Census 2001.* London: Directgov. Retrieved November 27, 2009, from http://www.statistics.gov.uk/census2001/census2001.asp.

Office for National Statistics. (2001b). *Ethnic minorities in Birmingham based on ward profiles.* Retrieved November 27, 2009, from http://www.statistics.gov.uk/census2001/profiles/00cn.asp.

Omaar, R. (2008, April 11). Immigration, the inconvenient truth: A dangerous fragmentation. *Dispatches.* UK: Channel 4.

Open Society Institute (2005). *Muslims in the UK: Policy for engaged citizenship.* Budapest: Open Society Institute.

Parry, J. (2004). *What is multiculturalism and how can sport relate to multiculturalist goals?* Paper presented at the Sport in Promoting Multicultural Understanding and the Social integration of Migrant Groups in Europe, Paris.

Ramadan, T. (2002). *Musulmans d'occident: Construire et Contribuer.* Paris: Tawhid.

Ramadan, T. (2004). *Western Muslims and the future of Islam.* London: Oxford University Press.

Robinson, F. (1988). *Varieties of South Asian Islam.* Warwick: University of Warwick, Centre for Research in Ethnic Relations.

Saheli Women's Group (Writer). (2006). Saheli activities film: Saheli adventure hub [DVD]. In R. Smith (Producer), http://www.community-film-maker.org.uk.

Said, E. (1991). *Orientalism: western conceptions of the Orient.* London: Penguin.

Sardar, Z. (2006, July 2). A question of identity. *The Observer.* Retrieved July 2, 2006, from http://www.guardian.co.uk/sport/2006/jul/02/cricket.features1.

Sardar, Z. (2008, September 25). Who are the British Asians? *New Statesman.* Retrieved September 30, 2008, from http://www.newstatesman.com/uk-politics/2008/09/british-asians-britain-india.

Silverstein, P. (2002). Stadium politics: sport, Islam and Amazigh consciousness in France and North Africa. In T. Magdalinski, & C. Jlt (Eds.), *With God on their side, sport in the service of religion* (pp. 37–70). London: Routledge.

Sisters Games. (2009). Sisters Games—Sports in Birmingham for sisters-only. Birmingham: Ummah.com—Mulsim Forum. Retrieved November 10, 2009, from http://www.ummah.com/forum/showthread.php?t=206778.

Sport England. (2002). *No limits: Sport England's equity policy*. London: Sport England.

Sport England. (2005). *New guidance in the design of sport facilities*. London: Sport England.

Sport England. (2007). *Sport England equality scheme*. London: Sport England.

Sport England. (2009). *The active people survey*. Retrieved November 1, 2009, from http://www.sportengland.org/index/get_resources/research/active_people.htm.

Stodolska, M., & Livengood, J. (2006). The effects of religion on the leisure behaviour of American Muslim immigrants. *Journal of Leisure Research*, *38*, 293–320.

Sturcke, J. (2006, October 6). Straw: I'd rather no one wore veils. *Guardian*. Retrieved October 7, 2006, from http://www.guardian.co.uk/politics/2006/oct/06/immigrationpolicy.religion.

Taylor, T., & Toohey, K. (2002). Behind the veil: Exploring the recreation needs of Muslim women. *Leisure Studies, 26, 85–105.*

UK Sport (2001, 2002, 2003). *Equality and diversity strategy; The government's plan for sport*. London: UK Sport.

Walseth, K. (2006a). Sport and belonging. *International Review for the Sociology of Sport*, *41*(3–4), 447–464.

Walseth, K. (2006b). Young Muslim women and sport: The impact of identity work. *Leisure Studies*, *25*(1), 75–94.

Wodak, R., De Cillia, R., Blüml, K., & Andraschko, E. (1989). *Language and power—Language and politics. The contribution of linguistics to civic education*. Vienna: Deuticke.

Wolman, H., & Ford, C. (1996). The assumptive world of local political elites. *Urban Affairs Review*, *32*, 87–108.

Young, K. (1977). Values in the policy process. *Policy and Politics*, *5*, 1–22.

Zaman, H. (1997). Islam, well-being and physical activity: Perceptions of Muslim young women. In G. Clarke & B. Humberstone (Eds.), *Researching women and sport* (pp. 50–67). London: Macmillan.

Cross-sectoral Variation in Organizational Culture in the Fitness Industry

ERIC W. MACINTOSH*, ALISON DOHERTY** & MATT WALKER†

*Human Kinetics, University of Ottawa, Ottawa, Canada; **Kinesiology, University of Western Ontario, London, Canada & †Sport Management Program, University of Florida, Gainesville, USA

ABSTRACT This study compared the perception and impact of organizational culture on staff working in for-profit and non-profit organizations in the fitness industry. The purpose was to examine whether there was any variation in the emphasis on certain values within these organizations which may distinguish the sectors of this competitive industry. The study also considered whether there were differences in the impact of certain values on employee behavior. Survey research was employed during a major fitness conference and trade show that organizations from both sectors attend. Data were gathered from 416 fitness industry staff, of which 209 worked in the for-profit sector while 60 worked in the non-profit sector. The findings revealed that cross-sectoral variation in organizational culture was limited to the greater emphasis placed on sales in for-profit organizations. The findings suggest that shared values exist within an industry. Findings also showed that a focus on sales in both sectors increased staff intention to leave, while connectedness was inversely associated with intention to leave in the non-profit sector only. Directions for future research on the variation and impact of organizational culture are presented.

Cross-sectoral Variation in Organizational Culture in the Fitness Industry

Organizational culture is typically conceptualized as the values, beliefs and basic assumptions that help guide and control member behavior and is, therefore, considered to be a micro-phenomenon that is specific to an organization (Martin, 1992; Sackmann, 2001; Schein, 1985). Research has elucidated that organizational culture has a significant impact on staff attitudes and behaviors, making it one of the most important management theories to comprehend (Allen, 2006; Goffee & Jones, 1996; Silverthorne, 2004). Despite the acknowledgement that organizational culture is specific to a company, there is merit in examining culture from an industry-wide perspective. This idea is important since the external environment in which organizations operate may be a key determinant in the formation of salient values and beliefs (Choi & Scott, 2008; Ogbonna & Harris, 2002; Smith & Shilbury, 2004; Velliquette & Rapert, 2001). Values and beliefs may be shaped by common demands and dynamics, which may be similar across organizations in an industry (Lee & Yu, 2004). There is evidence of (in some cases unique) industry-wide cultures within several industries, including food retail (Ogbonna & Harris, 2002), high tech manufacturing, health care and insurance (Lee & Yu, 2004), sport (Choi & Scott, 2008; Smith & Shilbury, 2004) and, most notably, fitness (MacIntosh & Doherty, 2010).

Various environmental forces cause organizations to adopt and adapt certain ways of doing things (Dickson, Aditya, & Chhokar, 2000; Skinner, Stewart, & Edwards, 1999). This idea is consistent with institutional theory whereby an industry can influence organizational practices (DiMaggio & Powell, 1983; Lounsbury, 2001; Slack & Parent, 2006). Organizations change to "... conform with expectations in their institutional environment" (Slack & Parent, 2006, p. 242) and to be like other organizations (and their structures and systems) that have been deemed to be successful.

In sport management, O'Brien and Slack (1999) discussed how values such as amateurism (i.e. within an English rugby union Premiership club) are accepted based on the history and tradition of the games and are thus institutionalized. However, due to environmental forces (e.g. social, political) these values can evolve and change to fit new circumstances. Skinner et al. (1999) argued that environmental forces can result in complex changes to values that filter through organizations at different rates of speed. According to Zakus and Skinner (2008), there is evidence of environmental forces changing values within the International Olympic Committee (IOC). In particular, the authors found new values (e.g. transparent commercial focus) emerged within the IOC as a result of the commercial viability, corruption and ethical scandals surrounding the Salt Lake City Olympic Games.

According to DiMaggio and Powell (1983), the pressure to compete and survive forces organizations to take notice of successful organizational structures and processes. Furthermore, best practices of organizations that have experienced success can diffuse across an industry through the various networks that organizations share, resulting in replication. Replication of organizational structures and processes has been found in a variety of contexts due to environmental pressures and competition (Lawrence & Suddaby, 2006). The practice of replication or imitation may be particularly common in the fitness industry, where clubs offer comparable fitness programming (e.g. step-classes, spin-classes, mind-body classes) and amenities (e.g. change rooms, lockers) (Alexandris, Zahariadis, Tsorbatzoudis, & Grouios, 2004; Chang & Lee, 2004). The existence of an industry-wide culture is another indication of pressure to adopt common values, beliefs and assumptions that guide daily practices in fitness organizations (MacIntosh & Doherty, 2008).

However, the idea of a dominant culture comprising the values and beliefs that is common across an industry leaves open the possibility of existing subcultures within that industry (MacIntosh & Doherty, 2008; Martin, 1992), where particular values are more important in some subsets of the industry than others. One possible basis of variation is industry sector—specifically, non-profit and for-profit organizations. Different mandates and stakeholder expectations in these two sectors may engender different values and ways of doing things, despite imitation of fitness programs and services (e.g. Rose-Ackerman, 1990; Ulseth, 2004).

Cross-sectoral variation with regard to commercial vs. non-commercial activity, service quality, adoption of technology, human resource management, social integration of members and survival has been considered in the context of hospitals (e.g. Chakravarty, Gaynor, Klepper, & Vogt, 2006; Gaynor & Vogt, 2003; Sloan, 1998), long-term care facilities (e.g. Ben-Ner, Flint Paulson, & Ren, 2009; Hirth, 1997, 1999), sport and leisure facilities (MacVicar & Ogden, 2001; Ulseth, 2004), and for-profit and non-profit organizations in general (Lakdawalla & Philipson, 2006; Rose-Ackerman, 1990). According to Rose-Ackerman (1990, p. 13),

> Non-profits and for-profits coexist in the same industry when each type of firm can find a stable market niche that rewards its own special strengths: ideological commitment in the non-profit sector; access to capital and the profit motive in the for-profit.

These distinct ideologies are thought to be reflected in "... firm-level differences in the behavior and objectives of nonprofits and for-profits" (Lakdawalla & Philipson, 2006, p. 1683) Lakdawalla and Philipson (2006, p. 1683) further noted that industry performance is dependent on organizations that are not completely homogeneous nor "... perfectly competitive". Although the non-profit (e.g. YMCA) and for-profit sectors (e.g. LA Fitness) are recognized subsets of the fitness industry (Fitness Business Canada, 2009; Mintel International Group, 2009), there is a considerable lack of research on cross-sectoral variation in this context. Knowledge of any variation between for-profit and non-profit fitness organizations may provide insight into any competitive advantage one sector has over the other, particularly with regard to retaining employees and clients, both of which are critical issues in this industry (Bishop, 2008; McCarthy, 2004).

This paper stems from a larger investigation of organizational culture in the fitness industry (MacIntosh & Doherty, 2010). Accordingly, the primary purpose of this research was to examine whether there is cross-sectoral variation in what has previously been identified as an industry-wide culture (MacIntosh & Doherty, 2008), with a specific focus on for-profit and non-profit fitness organizations. The secondary purpose was to examine whether there is variation in the impact of organizational culture on employee behavior in for-profit and non-profit fitness organizations. The impact of organizational culture on employee attitudes and behavior has been widely noted (Allen, 2006; Egan, Yang & Bartlett, 2004; Silverthorne, 2004), including in the fitness industry (MacIntosh et al., 2010; MacIntosh & Doherty, 2005). One of the best methods for predicting employee turnover is examining behavioral intentions (Maertz & Campion, 1998). Given the intents of this research, this work contributes to the extant literature in several ways. First, the findings add to the growing body of research on the fitness industry in sport management (Alexandris et al., 2004; Bodet, 2006; Chang & Lee, 2004; Hurley, 2004; MacIntosh & Doherty, 2008; MacVicar & Ogden, 2001). Secondly, the examination of subcultures based on industry sector enhances our general understanding of industry-wide culture in the fitness domain and in general (cf. Ashkanasy, Broadfoot, & Falkus, 2000; Martin, 1992). Thirdly, the findings increase our understanding of the impact of organizational culture on staff behavioral intentions (Maertz & Campion, 1998). In order to satisfy these purposes, the researchers utilized a quantitative approach whereby a questionnaire was administered to a sample of fitness industry employees in both sectors during a major Canadian fitness conference and trade show.

This paper is organized into several sections. The following section provides an overview of the Canadian fitness industry with respect to its growth and size, a description of its for-profit and non-profit sectors, and the connection to sport management. A review of the theoretical framework follows, including notably a description of how organizational culture and subcultures are defined in this study and an overview of cross-sectoral variation examined in other research.

The Canadian Fitness Industry

In Canada, the late 1970s and early 1980s marked the period of remarkable exposure regarding the benefits of regular weight-bearing and cardiovascular exercise. During this time period, the fitness industry began a metamorphosis whereby "regular gyms" (e.g. weight bench, bar bells, dumb bells etc.) evolved to include more advanced machinery for exercise training purposes (e.g. nautilus equipment), and where more of a focus was placed on meeting consumer demand for state-of-the-art facilities. Indeed, exercise was being viewed as important for the regular person and no longer the domain of weightlifters or athletes (Spanning 25 Years: IDEA and Fitness Industry Milestones, 2007).

In the mid-1980s, fitness organizations began offering exercise classes to persons at all levels of fitness under the same roof. Group exercise proved to be a valued service in both sectors, providing new opportunities for exercisers to self-challenge as well as more marketable programs to attract greater numbers of people seeking new types of programming (e.g. spin classes, step classes, etc.). The later part of the 1980s also brought forth a relatively new service of one-to-one personal training (Spanning 25 Years:

IDEA and Fitness Industry Milestones, 2007). This service offered members expert advice on exercise routines while providing additional revenue streams. At that point, the burgeoning fitness industry began to be met with criticism from concerned consumer groups as a result of the lack of a professional body to oversee how the industry operated, particularly related to membership fees (Perusse, 1992; Wolff, 1987). This type of external pressure began to challenge the status quo regarding fitness policies and pricing of memberships within organizations. In an effort to self-regulate, provincial organizations (e.g. the Saskatchewan Parks and Recreation Association) began offering certification to fitness personnel through the National Fitness Leadership Alliance starting in 1985 (Get SPRA Certified, 2010). In 1993, the organization of Canadian Fitness Professionals was born to be the voice of fitness professionals and act as an educational and certification body for personal trainers and exercise instructors across the country in both sectors (CanFitPro, 2010).

The attempt to legitimize the service offerings in the industry was supported by the Canadian Fitness Safety Standards which were first developed in 1990, and later reviewed, revised and republished in 2000 and 2004 (Canadian Fitness Safety Standards, 2004). Today, this initiative is a program within the Canada Safety Council. In addition, the formation of the organization Fitness Industry Canada, which acts in part to create an equal playing field for fitness organizations and lobbies the Canadian government to provide tax incentives for people that are active (e.g. Children's Fitness Tax Credit; www.english.ficdn.ca/), has lent further credence to the growth of the industry in terms of more formalized control mechanisms. As of 2006, the industry is said to comprise over 4,700 fitness organizations across the country (McNeil, 2006) and continues to be in a period of rapid expansion with respect to club growth (Mintel International Group, 2006).

Varying types of organizations operate in the Canadian fitness industry. The broadest distinction can be made between those in the for-profit sector (e.g. GoodLife Fitness Clubs Inc.) and those in the non-profit sector (e.g. YMCA). For-profit organizations (as their name entails) have a mandate to maximize profit and distribute funds to the ownership, while those in the non-profit sector (also as their name entails) have a mandate to break even or use any surplus revenues to improve services and programming to benefit the membership and community (Chelladurai, 2009). Another distinguishing feature of for-profit and non-profit organizations is the preferential regulatory or tax treatment that non-profit organizations realize (Lakdawalla & Philipson, 2006). Non-profits are also more likely to receive monetary and in-kind subsidy; however, they are less likely to have access to equity capital (Rose-Ackerman, 1990). As a result, non-profit organizations may have "... weaker incentives than for-profits to be productively efficient" (Rose-Ackerman, 1990, p. 15), yet they often have higher levels of formalization and rule enforcement due to having to answer to governing bodies and other agencies and interest groups (Rainey & Bozeman, 2000).

A report from the Mintel International Group (2006) indicated that close to half of fitness organizations are for-profit (45%), whereas non-profit organizations comprise approximately 38% of the North American industry. Other organizations falling under the miscellaneous category are corporate facilities, hotel, church-based and military facilities (Mintel International Group, 2006). Further, 53% of the fitness industry work force is employed with for-profit organizations (Mintel International Group, 2006). These organizations rely heavily on income derived from membership sales and ancillary services, such as pro-shops, tanning beds, and food and beverage sales as well as membership services such as personal training revenues (Mintel International Group, 2009). In contrast, non-profit fitness organizations rely in part on private donations and government funding as well as membership income to aid their operations (e.g. YMCA, 2008). Illustrating this point, in one community-based report, YMCA revenues which totaled in excess of CA$3 million for membership sales comprised less than one-third (28.8%) of revenues for that operating year (YMCA, 2001). Non-profit fitness organizations are also able to reduce their operating expenses with tax subsidies.

As mentioned, organizations in the for-profit and non-profit sectors of the fitness industry have (by definition) divergent mandates (MacVicar & Ogden, 2001). They are also likely to be distinguished by features consistent with for-profit and non-profit organizations in general, as described above. Thus, we may expect there to be cross-sectoral variation in the values and beliefs that reflect how things are done in these types of fitness organizations. However, non-profits in the fitness industry still need to attract and retain customers, and thus find themselves involved in what could be considered more commercial activities (cf. Rose-Ackerman, 1990; Schiff & Weisbrod, 1991). Similarly, competition from the non-profit organizations may place more pressure on the for-profit organizations to deliver socially beneficial services to communities in an effort to appear committed to societal welfare (Hirth, 1997). This intersection of for-profit and non-profit fitness organizations suggests we may expect cross-sectoral similarities in what is valued and how things are done in those organizations.

Certainly, the ability of fitness organizations to survive in this competitive industry requires an emphasis on the service environment (e.g. MacIntosh & Doherty, 2007). The belief that providing high levels of customer service will increase member satisfaction and thus produce higher rates of return for fitness organizations is widely shared amongst industry leaders (McCarthy, 2004). This sentiment has been both implicitly assumed as well as empirically verified; in that service quality (e.g. equipment, programmes, facilities, ancillary services) has been found to be of the utmost importance to both for-profit and non-profit fitness organizations (Cavnar, Kirtland, Evans, Wilson, Williams, Mixon, & Henderson, 2004; MacIntosh & Doherty, 2007). Further, Lagrosen and Lagrosen (2007) reported that management practices with respect to service quality appear to be similar across the industry, although possible cross-sectoral variation was not a focus of their study. In general, the fitness industry continues to evolve as educational standards and certifications have become more apparent in organizational operations within both sectors. In addition, the industry has developed a greater sense of the importance of professionalized services in both the non-profit and for-profit organizations.

Concomitantly, Chelladurai (2005, p. 49) noted that the fitness industry is linked to sport management, which he defined as "a field concerned with the coordination of limited human and material resources, relevant technologies, and situational contingencies for the efficient production and exchange of sport services". Fitness organizations are classified in the category of sport participant services (as distinct from sport spectator services), offering consumers an opportunity to meet their pleasure and/or health and fitness needs through any or all of skill development, pursuit of excellence, sustenance and healing/restoration (Chelladurai, 2005). As such, fitness organizations can benefit from the examination of the coordination of resources, technologies and situational contingencies for the efficient production and exchange of their particular sport participant services. Indeed, research on fitness club management focusing on service quality for members and, to a lesser extent, a quality environment for employees, has been a mainstay of the sport management literature (e.g. Alexandris et al., 2004; Bodet, 2006; Chang & Lee, 2004; MacIntosh & Doherty, 2007). Research on the fitness industry provides insight into this segment of the broader sport industry and management of this category of sport services in particular.

Theoretical Framework

When organizations form, core values and beliefs emerge based on founding principles and ways of doing things (Schein, 1991). Over time, the ongoing negotiation and practices of group members who enter the organization further shape the values and beliefs central to organizational life, and inform both acceptable and unacceptable ways of how jobs are performed (Kusluvan & Karamustafa, 2003; Tyrrell, 2000). For this study, we followed the view of Schein (1991) who conceptualized organizational culture as the important values, beliefs and basic assumptions that guide organizational life and, in part, explain why an organization is the way that it is. Schein (1991) further argued that the common everyday practices are manifestations of what is most important and tend to reinforce the basic principles of why an organization exists.

Elements of organizational culture can form and evolve to fit industry dynamics and demands (Lee & Yu, 2004), similar to DiMaggio and Powell's (1983) idea that organizations will develop similarities since they face comparable pressures to legitimize and survive. Slack and Hinings (1994) argued that when organizations face institutional pressures that emanate from regulatory bodies who require changes to structure, they adopt similar strategies to ensure success. Correspondingly, Leiter (2005) noted that institutional pressures and the pressure to compete will influence organizations working in different sectors of the economy (i.e. non-profit, for-profit) within the same industry to adopt similar ways of doing things. As a consequence, organizations are likely to replicate some best practices for long-term survival, as well as values and beliefs that guide organizational life. This manifestation could partially explain the existence of industry-wide organizational culture (e.g. Chatman & Jehn, 1994; MacIntosh & Doherty, 2008; Ogbonna & Harris, 2002).

None the less, the idea that members of an organization (or industry members) think and act alike, and share a common understanding of the values and beliefs may be idealistic (Slack & Parent, 2006). As Martin (1992) suggested, it is likely that individuals, groups and organizations differ with respect to the intensity of shared values or even the nature of those values. This differentiation perspective is the basis of organizational subcultures (Martin, 1992). Such subcultures are thought to occur as a result of a number of different factors including similar demographics, common experiences and problems (Slack & Parent, 2006). Southall (2001) found evidence of subcultures based on revenue and non-revenue sports within university athletic departments, and MacIntosh and Doherty (2005) uncovered subcultures according to employees of head office and club staff in one fitness organization. Research has alluded to the various ways in which people and groups differ from the dominant culture paradigm. According to Martin's (1992) differentiation perspective, a subculture supports the dominant values (i.e. enhancing), denies the dominant values (i.e. countering) or simply exists alongside the dominant culture (i.e. orthogonal). Given these possible subculture permutations within a dominant culture, it is of interest to examine whether there is variation in certain values among different types of organizations within a single industry. Ashkanasy et al. (2000) argued that an industry-wide organizational culture permits such cross-sectional comparisons. Given this commentary, the focus of this study is cross-sectoral variation in the perceived culture of for-profit and non-profit fitness organizations. An additional consideration was cross-sectoral variation in the impact of values on employee behavior and, more specifically, intention to leave, since research has shown that organizational culture has a significant influence in this regard (e.g. Egan, Yang, & Bartlett, 2004; MacIntosh & Doherty, 2005; Maertz & Campion, 1998). In addition, we sought to examine how values influenced employees of the different sectors in light of the identified industry problems relating to staff retention.

Method

Instrument

The questionnaire comprised the Culture Index for Fitness Organizations (CIFO) previously created to examine employee perceptions of cultural dimensions or underlying core values of daily organizational life in the Canadian fitness industry (MacIntosh & Doherty, 2010). Thirty-nine items representing eight dimensions of industry-wide culture in the fitness domain were examined: *staff competency* (knowledge, credentials, positive attitude;

$n = 9$ items); *atmosphere* (club is welcoming, upbeat, fun; $n = 7$ items); *connectedness* (sense of affiliation, belonging in the club, recognition of members; $n = 5$ items); *formalization* (club has policies, procedures, standards; $n = 5$ items); *sales* (emphasized, rewarded, $n = 4$ items); *service equipment* (good variety, quality, availability; $n = 3$ items); *service programs* (current, innovative, varied; $n = 3$ items); and *organizational presence* (club has long history, positive image; $n = 3$ items). Participants were asked to rate on a Likert-type scale of 1 (strongly disagree) to 7 (strongly agree) whether they felt the items represented how things are within their fitness organization. All of the factors were found to be internally consistent based on Cronbach's alpha scores and were determined to be relatively independent based on intercorrelation values that indicated that multicollinearity was not problematic (Tabachnick & Fidell, 2007).

The questionnaire also included a measure of work-related behavior (i.e. intention to leave). Three items were developed as part of the larger investigation (MacIntosh & Doherty, 2010) to measure participants' intention to leave their organization. Two of the items (How often have you felt like quitting your job? How often have you felt like leaving your organization?) were rated on a scale of 1 (never) to 7 (often). The third item (How long do you think you will stay with your organization?) was rated on a scale of 1 (will leave very soon) to 7 (will stay forever) and was reversed scored. The Cronbach's alpha reliability coefficient was acceptable for the intention to leave measure (alpha $= 0.81$), according to the criteria posited by Lance, Butts, and Michels (2006). Participants were also asked to identify the sector within which they worked (for-profit, non-profit) as well as demographic information (i.e. gender, age, tenure in their organization) in order to develop a participant profile. In order to achieve 90% confidence that the sample and population percentages would not differ more than 5%, a minimum of 350 completed surveys were recommended (Baumgartner, Strong, & Hensley, 2002).

Participants and Procedure

The questionnaire was administered during a major Canadian fitness conference and trade show attended by employees of organizations in both the for-profit and non-profit sectors of the industry. This strategy was advantageous since the researchers knew specific characteristics (i.e. gender and age) of the population of interest that would be attending the event and were able to collect data through an accessible cohort that gathered at one place over a short period of time, thus meeting the intent of the investigation (Baumgartner et al., 2002). It was estimated that approximately 4,000 delegates would be attending the conference based on the previous years' registration (R. Macdonald, personal communication). Information from the trade-show host indicated that approximately 98% of delegates would be Canadian, 8 out of 10 would be female and the average age of delegates would be approximately 36 years. It was known that employees from fitness organizations in both the for-profit and non-profit sectors attend the trade show; however, the percentage of those in attendance that worked in each sector was unknown.

To recruit participants and collect data, the researchers had an onsite booth where the questionnaires were administered. The researchers' booth was located on the main floor of the trade show and was surrounded by fitness and other organizations (e.g. nutrition, apparel) that were displaying various products and services. The booth displayed a sign that announced "Research Study on the Canadian Fitness Industry". Delegates who approached the booth were greeted and offered a letter of information which outlined the study and explained their rights as a potential research participant. If meeting the primary criterion for inclusion (i.e. working in the Canadian fitness industry) and upon their agreement to participate in the research, the individuals were provided with the questionnaire and asked to return the completed questionnaire onsite to the booth or (if they felt so inclined) return it by mail using the provided self-addressed stamped envelope. Participants were also invited to fill out a ballot for an opportunity to win draw prizes, such as one of two MP3 players. The ballots with the participant's name and contact information were separated from the completed surveys to ensure anonymity of the data.

During a period of three days, a total of 612 questionnaires were distributed to delegates. The highest traffic during the first day occurred early in the morning, whereas on days two and three traffic was highest during the early afternoon. In total, 392 (91%) surveys were collected onsite and 40 (9%) were returned by mail within two weeks of the conference. In total, 416 were deemed useable, for a final response rate of 68%. The current paper is based on a sample of 269 participants who indicated whether they were employed in the for-profit or non-profit sector.

In terms of the sample's demography, women comprised 82% of the respondent pool ($n = 221$). The average age of respondents was 33 years ($SD = 10.4$), and the average tenure with their fitness organization was two years ($SD = 0.78$). Overall, 77% ($n = 209$) of the respondents were from for-profit organizations and 23% ($n = 60$) were from non-profit organizations. With respect to gender and age, the study sample is comparable to the profile of delegates at the conference and fitness industry personnel on the whole, according to labor force data (US Department of Labor, 2007) and is consistent with other fitness industry research (MacIntosh & Doherty, 2005). However, the sample appears to be over-represented based on sector according to the Mintel International Group (2006) report that 53% of employees in the fitness industry work in for-profit organizations. Given this, caution should be taken in the interpretation of the study findings.

Results

Cross-sectoral Subcultures

A 2×8 analysis of variance (ANOVA) with repeated measures on the eight cultural dimensions was used to determine if differences existed between employees' perceptions of organizational culture in for-profit and non-profit fitness organizations. The results showed a significant main effect for industry sector, $F(1, 267) = 8.62$, $p < 0.05$. Results of further univariate analyses revealed that only the cultural dimension of *sales* was perceived to be significantly different in the two sectors ($p < 0.001$), where *sales* were apparently a greater focus in for-profit organizations (Table 1). No other significant differences by industry sector were found regarding the employees' perceptions of organizational culture.

Cross-sectoral Impact of Organizational Culture

Given that sector was a dichotomous variable (i.e. for-profit, non-profit), it was not possible to directly examine its moderating effect on the impact of organizational culture on employees' intent to leave their organization (Todman & Dugard, 2007). Rather, correlation analyses and comparisons of the independent and dependent variable at each level of the moderator was possible and deemed appropriate (Todman & Dugard, 2007). Following the correlation analyses and to examine the unique contribution of significant variables, standard linear regression was employed. Linear regression treats variables as competing in explaining variation amongst outcomes (Newton & Rudestam, 1999) and subsequently provides the unique contribution of each variable in the equation (Fiss, 2007).

The results of bivariate correlation analyses between each of the cultural dimensions and intent to leave for both sectors are presented in Table 2. An inverse relationship suggests that the more a value is realized, the less likely staff will quit. As seen in Table 2, for-profit employees' intent to leave the organization was significantly and directly associated with the values of *sales*, and inversely associated with *staff competency*, *atmosphere*, *connectedness* and *service programs*. Non-profit employees' intent to leave their organization was significantly and directly associated with the values of *sales*, and inversely associated with *connectedness* and *service programs*.

Table 1. Descriptive (mean (M), standard deviation (SD)) and comparative (univariate F) statistics for cultural dimensions by industry sector

	For-profit		Non-profit		
Cultural dimensions	M	SD	M	SD	F (1, 267)
Sales	5.88	1.11	3.72	1.37	156.12*
Staff competency	5.40	1.02	5.54	0.74	1.06
Atmosphere	5.77	1.01	5.77	0.73	0.00
Connectedness	5.20	1.20	5.09	0.92	0.44
Formalization	5.34	1.13	5.23	0.89	0.59
Service equipment	5.48	1.29	5.34	0.80	0.64
Service programs	5.73	1.10	5.51	0.99	1.92
Organizational presence	5.46	1.06	5.53	1.15	0.20

*$p < 0.001$

Table 2. Correlations (r) between cultural dimensions and intent to leave for employees in the for-profit and non-profit sectors

Cultural dimension	For-profit	Non-profit
Sales	0.17**	0.29*
Staff competency	−0.17**	−0.28
Atmosphere	−0.17**	−0.13
Connectedness	−0.13*	−0.23*
Formalization	0.06	0.17
Service equipment	−0.09	0.23
Service programs	−0.12*	−0.22*
Organizational presence	0.00	−0.02

**$p < 0.001$, *$p < 0.05$

Based on the above findings, separate standard regression analyses were conducted for intent to leave among employees in the for-profit and the non-profit industry sectors. In order to maintain statistical power (i.e. by minimizing the number of independent variables), the analyses were based on only those cultural dimensions that were found to be significantly correlated with intent to leave in each sector. Therefore, the regressions examined the impact of *sales*, *staff competency*, *atmosphere*, *connectedness* and *service programs* in the for-profit sector, while the impact of *sales*, *connectedness* and *service programs* were examined in the non-profit sector. The maximum variance inflation factor (VIF) was 5.62 for the for-profit model and 4.87 for the non-profit model, indicating that multicollinearity of the independent variables in each model was not problematic, as they were below the critical threshold of 10 (Belsley, Kuh, & Welsch, 1980). Consequently, it was deemed appropriate to continue with interpretation of the regression results (Table 3). In the for-profit sector, the relationship with the cultural dimension of *sales* ($\beta = 0.25$; $p < 0.001$) made the only significant contribution to the prediction of intention to leave ($F(5, 203) = 3.61$; $p < 0.005$). The findings indicated that together the cultural dimensions explained 8.2% of the variance. In the non-profit sector, both *sales* ($\beta = 0.34$, $p < 0.01$) and *connectedness* ($\beta = -0.27$ $p < 0.05$) made unique contributions to the prediction of intent to leave ($F(3, 56) = 4.33$; $p < 0.01$), and the cultural dimensions together explained 18.8% of the variance.

Discussion

The findings suggest minimal cross-sectoral variation with regard to perceived organizational culture in the Canadian fitness industry. This provides some further evidence of a dominant industry-wide culture in the fitness domain. In addition, our work revealed fairly strong agreement among employees in for-profit and non-profit organizations that the cultural dimensions examined here represent what is valued and how things are done

Table 3. Regression analyses of select cultural dimensions on intent to leave in the for-profit and non-profit sectors

Cultural dimension	β	F	R^2
For-profit sector			
Staff competency	−0.02	3.612 (4)	0.082
Atmosphere	−0.14		
Connectedness	−0.01		
Sales	0.25***		
Service programs	−0.11		
Non-profit sector			
Connectedness	−0.27*	4.334 (2)	0.188
Sales	0.34**		
Service program	−0.13		

$^*p < 0.05$, $^{**}p < 0.01$, $^{***}p < 0.001$

in both sectors, with one exception—*sales*. *Sales* were perceived to be significantly stronger by employees in the for-profit sector. The relatively greater focus on *sales* in for-profit fitness organizations is perhaps not surprising given the different financial mandates in the two sectors. With for-profit organizations, revenue maximization is the goal of operations, with the intent of generating income for the owners (Chelladurai, 2009; Rose-Ackerman, 1990). These organizations rely entirely on sales to survive. Conversely, non-profit organizations have a mandate to break even financially with any surplus revenues turned back into the organization (Chelladurai, 2009; Rose-Ackerman, 1990). These divergent mandates are reflected in the extent to which the cultural dimension of *sales* is perceived to be a major focus of the organization. Lakdawalla and Philipson (2006) argued that distinct ideologies would likely result in cross-sectoral differences in organizational objectives and behavior. To this end, for-profit organizations tend to have employees specifically tasked to obtain increased membership numbers, and rewarded further for sales related to ancillary services. In contrast, non-profit organizations typically have customer service employees that take walk-in sales but are not specifically tasked with selling as part of their job. The perceived greater emphasis on *sales* among employees in the for-profit fitness organizations in this study is also likely due to the relative importance of this revenue stream for organizational survival and success (see Rose-Ackerman, 1990).

The findings of this study suggest that, with the exception of *sales,* distinct subcultures do not exist by sector based on the cultural dimensions examined here. Instead, it appears that organizational culture within the for-profit and non-profit sectors enhances the dominant values of the fitness industry (Martin, 1992). For some of the dimensions, it was somewhat surprising that no cross-sectoral variation in employees' perceptions was observed. For example, research has posited that formalization in non-profit organizations may be higher since they have more constituents to report to, more rules to follow and more policies in place that inform acceptable work behaviors within organizations (Rainey & Bozeman, 2000). However, the current study suggests that organizations in both sectors were perceived to subscribe fairly heavily to *formalization*; specifically, policies and procedures, rules and regulations, staff grooming standards and staff training (MacIntosh & Doherty, 2010). As a result, it appears that this particular cultural dimension was perceived to be similar across the sectors and this may indeed be a function of the external pressures emanating across the industry for employee certification, safety standards and operating practices; a reflection of institutional pressures (Leiter, 2005).

No variation in the perception of *organizational presence* was also a surprising result given that this cultural dimension represents a focus on the image and importance of the organization within the community. One important mandate for non-profit organizations is to serve the community by fostering and growing programs and services that meet personal and social needs (e.g. health of community). It was notable that the image and presence of the organization in the community was perceived to be of equal focus by employees in for-profit and non-profit fitness organizations. This may be a function of competition from non-profit fitness organizations placing pressure on for-profit organizations to be more focused on their role in the community (see Hirth, 1997).

The findings also revealed no significant difference in the perception of *atmosphere*, suggesting that daily operations in for-profit and non-profit fitness organizations focus on creating a welcoming, upbeat and fun environment. This was not all that surprising given reports that management of fitness organizations need to focus on creating enjoyable environments for their clients to alleviate monotony with exercise routines (Mintel International Group, 2009). Employees were also similar in their perception of *connectedness* within their organizations, suggesting that there is a focus on creating a sense of affiliation and belonging in both sectors of the industry.

The results also suggest similar perceptions of both *service programs* and *service equipment*, highlighting the focus on the variety, quality and availability of equipment and variety and innovativeness of programs in fitness organizations in both sectors. These findings are consistent with the need for these organizations to be attuned to providing quality equipment, programs and services in order to achieve their mandate and survive (e.g. Cavnar et al., 2004; MacIntosh & Doherty, 2007) and complements the evidence that management practices with regards to service quality are similar across the industry (Lagrosen & Lagrosen, 2007).

The suggested evidence of an industry-wide culture in the fitness domain, with limited cross-sectoral variation, strengthens the argument that industry demands and dynamics shape the values, beliefs and underlying assumptions about how things are done in an organization within that industry (Choi & Scott, 2008; Lee & Yu, 2004; Ogbonna & Harris, 2002; Smith & Shilbury, 2004; Velliquette & Rapert, 2001). Consistent with institutional theory (Dickson et al., 2000; DiMaggio & Powell, 1983; Lounsbury, 2001), it appears that environmental forces may have caused fitness organizations to adopt and adapt certain ways of doing things across the industry, likely as a result of both regulation and competition, resulting in the replication and imitation of successful practices (DiMaggio & Powell, 1983; Lawrence & Suddaby, 2006; Leiter, 2005). Given such strong similarities, an argument can be made that the industry influences the values and beliefs operating across both sectors (Lounsbury, 2001; Slack & Parent, 2006). Perhaps one of the reasons why there appear to be such similarities is that both sectors compete for the same members. Hence, both sectors will engage in forms of replication (e.g. best practices and/or standards) in order to compete against one another. Within the fitness industry, certifications and regulations are ways in which fitness organizations can legitimize their service offerings to client-members. With high client-member turnover, and the competition for client-members (in general), catering to client-member demands (e.g. service quality) may have engendered an industry where the cultural dimensions of *atmosphere*, *connectedness*, *service equipment*, *service programs* are all key values present in daily operations. Further, both sectors interact through the same conferences and trade shows and thus are afforded ample opportunities to investigate innovative ways to improve operations. Fitness equipment and programming are large parts of the conference and trade-show circuit, with supplemental material relating to industry standards, education, and safety rules and regulations. Given such focus, it may not be surprising to find convergence with respect to the cultural dimensions examined.

The understanding of perceptible variation between for-profit and non-profit fitness organizations may offer insight into any competitive advantage one sector has over the other, particularly with regard to retaining employees and clients which have been noted to be of central concern for management in this industry (Bishop, 2008; McCarthy, 2004). Findings demonstrated that a focus on the cultural dimension of *sales* increased staff members' intention to leave the organization for both sectors. This suggests that an emphasis on *sales* may be precipitating issues with turnover in the fitness industry. Additionally, findings indicated that a lack of *connectedness* increased staff intention to leave non-profit organizations yet did not significantly influence staff in the for-profit sector. This nuance suggests that promoting a greater sense of staff affiliation and belonging to the club, while recognizing member accomplishments in the non-profit sector is more important for management and can be a method used to retain staff services longer. This particular finding is noteworthy because it includes an emphasis placed on celebrating the client-member. This may be an indication of ideal values at play in this sector since non-profit organizations exist to socially benefit community welfare (Hirth, 1997) and are not intended to maximize profit and distribute funds to the ownership as in the for-profit sector (Chelladurai, 2009). Thus, for non-profit staff, celebrating member success is a key tangible outcome to their feeling of accomplishment and overall sense of *connectedness* with the organization.

Lastly, several have argued that organizational culture influences corporate image (Hatch & Schultz, 1997; Kowalczyk & Pawlish, 2002) and there is evidence that clients do perceive organizational culture in the fitness industry

(MacIntosh & Doherty, 2007). However, the findings of the current study suggest that organizational culture is not a way that clients could distinguish fitness organizations in the different sectors (other than *sales*), and thus it is not a source of competitive advantage for those organizations in attracting clients. Hence, there are likely other organizational phenomena that differentiate organizations in the two sectors and explain why a client would choose one type of fitness organization over the other.

Conclusion and Limitations

In sum, our findings contribute to the growing body of research on the fitness industry (Alexandris et al., 2004; Bodet, 2006; Chang & Lee, 2004; Hurley, 2004; MacIntosh & Doherty, 2008; MacVicar & Ogden, 2001) and enhance our understanding of industry-wide culture and cross-sectoral variation. The findings suggest an industry-wide culture in the fitness domain based on the limited cross-sectoral variation in values and beliefs that guide staff behavior and organizational practice. However, the findings should be considered with caution as the sample was overrepresented by employees of for-profit organizations and was limited to those attending the conference and trade show. Although the numbers of delegates in attendance and the sub-samples by sector were sufficiently large to conduct the appropriate analyses, the under-representation of employees from non-profit organizations in this study should be acknowledged.

Another limitation was the focus on values and beliefs originally identified by fitness industry leaders and further refined by fitness professionals (MacIntosh & Doherty, 2008). Hence, there may be other cultural dimensions that are relevant to the study of industry subcultures, including dimensions that are part of orthogonal or counter-subcultures (Martin, 1992). These may be uncovered through further qualitative or mixed-methods work. Overall, further research is required to examine other possible cross-sectoral variations within the fitness industry, with the objective of understanding whether and how for-profit and non-profit organizations may be distinguished.

Future Research

Future research should examine whether there are subcultures in the fitness industry based on, for example, organizational size (e.g. large versus small client membership), organizational type (i.e. co-ed, hybrid, female only, fitness chain, independent fitness club) and job position within the organization itself (e.g. personal trainer, fitness instructor, management). These characteristics represent other ways that organizations in the fitness industry are distinguished and may be further examples which highlight similarities and differences. Exploring the possibility of subcultures according to these various levels of analysis, can further research on the fitness industry in general, and organizational culture in particular (Martin, 1992), with implications for a variety of management functions (e.g.

marketing, human resource practices). It would also be of interest to examine the perceptions of employees who have worked in both sectors of the fitness industry, thus uncovering any cultural similarities or differences from their perspective.

Further, a comparison of the perception of values in the fitness industry cross-culturally would be of interest, particularly since the fitness industry appears to be growing in multiple countries (Mintel International Group, 2006, 2009) and there is evidence that national culture influences organizational culture (Hampden-Turner & Trompenaars, 1993, 2000). Lastly, in order to continue to enhance our understanding of the fitness industry, it is also of interest to determine whether there is cross-sectoral variation in other elements of organizational life. For example, do facets of job satisfaction (e.g. employee compensation, job design, supervision, sales commission) help employees distinguish between for-profit and non-profit organizations in any meaningful way and further contribute to their retention? How does person-organization fit influence or predict turnover amongst the sectors? Can demographic information predict the various managerial outcomes related to staff retention?

Overall, the fitness industry is an important sector of the economy of several developed nations (e.g. UK, Canada, USA and Australia) and a key component of the field of sport management. Yet, much exploration and understanding remains regarding the organizations and personnel that support this growing industry.

References

Alexandris, K., Zahariadis, P., Tsorbatzoudis, C., & Grouios, G. (2004). An empirical investigation of the relationships among service quality, customer satisfaction and psychological commitment in a health club context. *European Sport Management Quarterly*, *4*(1), 36–52.

Allen, D.G. (2006). Do organizational socialization tactics influence newcomer embeddedness and turnover? *Journal of Management*, *32*, 237–256.

Ashkanasy, N.M., Broadfoot, L.E., & Falkus, S. (2000). Questionnaire measures of organizational culture. In N.M. Ashkanasy, C.P.M. Wilderom, & M.F. Peterson (Eds.), *Handbook of organizational culture and climate* (pp. 131–145). Thousand Oaks, CA: Sage.

Baumgartner, T.A., Strong, C.H., & Hensley, L.D. (2002). *Conducting and reading research in health and human performance* (3rd ed.). Boston: McGraw-Hill.

Belsley, D.A., Kuh, E., & Welsch, R.E. (1980). *Regression diagnostics: Identifying influential data and sources of collinearity*. New York: John Wiley & Sons.

Ben-Ner, A., Flint Paulson, D., & Ren, T. (2009, August). *Does ownership matter in the selection of nursing homes? Evidence from consumer surveys*. Paper presented at the 69th Academy of Management Conference, Chicago, IL.

Bishop, R. (2008, March). Why attrition numbers don't add up. *Fitness Management Magazine*. Retrieved October 19, 2009, from http://fitnessmanagement.com/articles/article.aspx?articleid=2347&zoneid=22.

Bodet, G. (2006). Investigating customer satisfaction in a health club context by an application of the Tetraclasse model. *European Sport Management Quarterly*, *6*, 149–165.

Canadian Fitness Safety Standards (2004). Retrieved March 8, 2010, from http://www.canadianfitnessmatters.ca/standards.

CanFitPro. (2010). Retrieved March 8, 2010, from http://www.humankinetics.com/ppCanFitPro.

Cavnar, M.M., Kirtland, K.A., Evans, M.H., Wilson, D.D., Williams, J.E., Mixon, G.M., & Henderson, K.A. (2004). Evaluating the quality of recreation facilities: Development of an assessment tool. *Journal of Park and Recreation Administration*, *22*(1), 96–114.

Chakravarty, S., Gaynor, M., Klepper, S., & Vogt, W.B. (2006). Does the profit motive make Jack nimble? Ownership form and the evolution of the US hospital industry. *Health Economics*, *15*, 345–361.

Chang, K., & Lee, C. (2004). Relationship among service quality, customer satisfaction, and renewal intentions in health/fitness clubs. *International Journal of Sport Management*, *5*, 306–315.

Chatman, J.A., & Jehn, K.A. (1994). Assessing the relationship between industry characteristics and organizational culture: How different can you be? *Academy of Management Journal*, *37*, 522–553.

Chelladurai, P. (2005). *Managing organizations for sport and physical activity: A systems perspective* (2nd ed.). Scottsdale, AZ: Holcomb Hathaway.

Chelladurai, P. (2009). *Managing organizations for sport and physical activity* (3rd ed.). Scottsdale, AZ: Holcomb Hathaway.

Choi, Y.S., & Scott, D.K. (2008). Assessing organizational culture using the competing values framework within American Triple-A baseball. *International Journal of Sport Management and Marketing*, *4*, 33–48.

Dickson, M.W., Aditya, R.N., & Chhokar, J.S. (2000). Definition and interpretation in cross-cultural organizational culture research. In N.M. Ashkanasy, C.P.M. Wilderom, & M.F. Peterson (Eds.), *Handbook of organizational culture and climate* (pp. 447–464). Thousand Oaks, CA: Sage.

DiMaggio, P.J., & Powell, W.W. (1983). The iron cage revisited: Institutional isomorphism and collective rationality in organization fields. *American Sociological Review*, *48*, 147–160.

Egan, T.M., Yang, B., & Bartlett, K. (2004). The effects of organizational learning culture and job satisfaction on motivation to transfer learning and turnover intention. *Human Resource Development Quarterly*, *15*, 279–301.

Fiss, P.C. (2007). A set-theoretic approach to organizational configurations. *Academy of Management Review*, *32*(4), 1180–1198.

Fitness Business Canada. (2009, October). *The magazine*. Retrieved November 12, 2009, from http://fitnet.ca/magazine.php.

Gaynor, M., & Vogt, W.B. (2003). Competition among hospitals. *Rand Journal of Economics*, *34*, 764–785.

Get SPRA Certified. (2010). Retrieved March 8, 2010, from http://www.spra.sk.ca/certification.

Goffee, R., & Jones, G. (1996). What holds the modern company together? *Harvard Business Review*, *74*(6), 133–148.

Hampden-Turner, C., & Trompenaars, F. (1993). *The seven cultures of capitalism*. London: Piarkus.

Hampden-Turner, C., & Trompenaars, F. (2000). *Building cross-cultural competence*. London: Yale University Press.

Hatch, M.J., & Schultz, M. (1997). Relations between organizational culture, identity and image. *European Journal of Marketing*, *31*, 356–365.

Hirth, R.A. (1997). Competition between for-profit and nonprofit health care providers: Can it help achieve social goals? *Medical Care Research and Review*, *54*(4), 414–438.

Hirth, R.A. (1999). Consumer information and competition between nonprofit and for-profit nursing homes. *Journal of Health Economics*, *18*, 219–240.

Hurley, T. (2004, September). Internal marketing and the effect on customer retention in the health and fitness industry. In *Proceedings of the 12th EASM European Congress on Sport Management* (pp. 156–158). Ghent, Belgium: PVLO.

Kowalczyk, S.J., & Pawlish, M.J. (2002). Corporate branding through external perception of organizational culture. *Corporate Reputation Review*, *5*(2), 159–174.

Kusluvan, Z., & Karamustafa, K. (2003). Organizational culture and its impacts on employee attitudes and behaviors in tourism and hospitality organizations. In S. Kusluvan (Ed.), *Managing employee attitudes and behaviors in the tourism and hospitality industry* (pp. 453–485). New York: Nova Science.

Lagrosen, S., & Lagrosen, Y. (2007). Exploring service quality in the health and fitness industry. *Managing Service Quality*, *17*(1), 41–53.

Lakdawalla, D., & Philipson, T. (2006). The nonprofit sector and industry performance. *Journal of Public Economics*, *90*, 1681–1698.

Lance, C.E., Butts, M.M., & Michels, L.C. (2006). The sources of four commonly reported cutoff criteria: What did they really say? *Organizational Research Methods*, *9*, 202.

Lawrence, T.B., & Suddaby, R. (2006). Institutions and institutional work. In S.R. Clegg, C. Hardy, T.B. Lawrence, & W.R. Nord (Eds.), *The SAGE handbook of organizational studies* (2nd ed.,) (pp. 215–254). Thousand Oaks, CA: Sage.

Lee, S.K.J., & Yu, K. (2004). Corporate culture and organizational performance. *Journal of Managerial Psychology*, *19*(4), 340–359.

Leiter, J. (2005). Structural isomorphism in Australian nonprofit organizations. *International Journal of Voluntary and Nonprofit Organizations*, *16*(1), 1–31.

Lounsbury, M. (2001). Institutional sources of practice variation: Staffing college and university recycling. *Administrative Science Quarterly*, *46*, 29–56.

MacIntosh, E., & Doherty, A. (2005). Leader intentions and employee perceptions of organizational culture in a private fitness corporation. *European Sport Management Quarterly*, *5*(1), 1–22.

MacIntosh, E., & Doherty, A. (2007). Reframing the service environment in the fitness industry. *Managing Leisure*, *12*, 273–289.

MacIntosh, E., & Doherty, A. (2008). Inside the Canadian fitness industry: Development of a conceptual framework of organizational culture. *International Journal of Sport Management*, *9*(3), 303–327.

MacIntosh, E., & Doherty, A. (2010). The influence of organizational culture on job satisfaction and intention to leave. *Sport Management Review*, *13*(2), 106–117, DOI: 10.1016/j.smr.2009.04.006.

MacVicar, A., & Ogden, S.M. (2001). Flexible working in sport and recreation: Current practices in Scottish public, not-for-profit and private leisure facilities. *Managing Leisure*, *6*, 125–140.

Maertz, C.P., & Campion, M.A. (1998). 25 years of voluntary turnover research: A review and critique. In C. Cooper, & I.T. Robertson (Eds.), *International review of industrial and organizational psychology* (pp. 49–81). New York: John Wiley & Sons.

Martin, J. (1992). *Cultures in organizations: Three perspectives*. New York: Oxford, University Press.

McCarthy, J. (2004). *Industry lessons and what, and what not to do*. Boston, MA: International Health, Racquet and Sportsclub Association.

McNeil, C.M. (2006). *State of the health club industry*. Boston, MA: International Health, Racquet and Sportsclub Association.

Mintel International Group. (2006, May). *Health and fitness clubs report*. Mintel International Group Limited.

Mintel International Group. (2009, October). *Health and fitness clubs—UK*. Mintel International Group Limited.

Newton, R.R., & Rudestam, K.E. (1999). *Your statistical consultant*. Thousand Oaks, CA: Sage.

O'Brien, D., & Slack, T. (1999). Deinstitutionalising the amateur ethic: An empirical examination of change in a rugby union football club. *Sport Management Review*, *2*, 24–42.

Ogbonna, E., & Harris, L.C. (2002). Organisational culture: A ten year, two-phase study of change in the UK food retailing sector. *Journal of Management Studies*, *39*, 673–706.

Perusse, B. (1992, March 19). Fitness fans getting the run around in quest for membership fee refunds. *The Gazette*, p. A3, Montreal, Quebec.

Rainey, H.G., & Bozeman, B. (2000). Comparing public and private organizations: Empirical research and the power of a priori. *Journal of Public Administration, Research and Theory*, *10*(2), 447–470.

Rose-Ackerman, S. (1990). Competition between non-profits and for-profits: Entry and growth. *Voluntas: International Journal of Voluntary and Nonprofit Organizations*, *1*(1), 13–25.

Sackmann, S. (2001). Cultural complexity in organizations: The value and limitations ofqualitative methodology and approaches. In C.L. Cooper, S. Cartwright, & P.C. Earley (Eds.), *International handbook of organizational culture and climate* (pp. 143–163). New York: John Wiley & Sons.

Schein, E.H. (1985). *Organizational culture and leadership*. San Francisco, CA: Jossey Bass.

Schein, E.H. (1991). The role of the founder in the creation of organizational culture. In P.J. Frost, L.F. Moore, M.R. Louis, C.C. Lundberg, & J. Martin (Eds.), *Reframing organizational culture* (pp. 14–25). Beverly Hills, CA: Sage.

Schiff, J., & Weisbrod, B. (1991). Competition between for-profit and nonprofit organizations in commercial markets. *Annals of Public and Cooperative Economics*, *62*(4), 619–640.

Silverthorne, C. (2004). The impact of organizational culture and person-organization fit on organizational commitment and job satisfaction in Taiwan. *Leadership & Organizational Development Journal*, *25*(7/8), 592–599.

Skinner, J., Stewart, B., & Edwards, A. (1999). Amateurism to professionalism: Modelling organisational change in sporting organisations. *Sport Management Review*, 2, 173–192.

Slack, T., & Hinings, B. (1994). Institutional pressures and isomorphic change: An empirical test. *Organization Studies*, *15*(6), 803–827.

Slack, T., & Parent, M.M. (2006). *Understanding sport organizations: the application of organization theory* (2nd ed.). Champaign, IL: Human Kinetics.

Sloan, F.A. (1998). Commericalism in nonprofit hospitals. *Journal of Policy Analysis and Management*, *17*, 234–252.

Smith, A., & Shilbury, D. (2004). Mapping cultural dimensions in Australian sporting organizations. *Sport Management Review*, *7*(2), 133–165.

Southall, R.M. (2001). *A study of organizational culture of Mountain West Conference intercollegiate athletic departments*. Paper presented at the Seventeenth Annual conference of the North American Society of Sport Management, Virginia Beach, VA.

Spanning 25 years: IDEA and fitness industry milestones 1982–2007. (2007, July/August). *IDEA Fitness Journal*, *4*(7), 24–35.

Tabachnick, & Fidell (2007). *Using multivariate statistics* (5th ed.). Boston, MA: Allyn and Bacon.

Todman, J., & Dugard, P. (2007). *Approaching multivariate analysis*. New York: Psychology Press.

Tyrrell, M.W.D. (2000). Hunting and gathering in the early silicon age. In N.M. Ashkanasy, C.P.M. Wilderom, & M.F. Peterson (Eds.), *Handbook of organizational culture and climate* (pp. 85–99). Thousand Oaks, CA: Sage.

Ulseth, A.B. (2004). Social integration in modern sport: Commercial fitness centres and voluntary sports clubs. *European Sport Management Quarterly*, *4*(2), 95–115.

US Department of Labor. (2007). *Women in the labor force: A data book* (report 1002). Washington, DC: US Department of Labor.

Velliquette, A., & Rapert, M. (2001). A profile of organizational culture: Implications for services marketing. *Services Marketing Quarterly*, *23*, 69–86.

Wolff, C. (1987, September 26). Going out of business: Clients come last. *The New York Times*. Retrieved November 12, 2009, from http://www.nytimes.com/1987/09/26/style/going-out-of-business-clients-come-last.html.

YMCA. (2001). *Building stronger communities: Report to the community 2001*. London, ON: YMCA.

YMCA. (2008). *Building momentum: Canada 2008 annual report*. Toronto, ON: YMCA.

Zakus, D.H., & Skinner, J. (2008). Modelling organizational change in the International Olympic Committee. *European Sport Management Quarterly*, *8*, 421–442.

A Culture of Trust: Engaging Muslim Women in Community Sport Organizations

HAZEL MAXWELL & TRACY TAYLOR

School of Leisure, Sport & Tourism, University of Technology, Sydney, Australia

ABSTRACT This article examines the impetus for, and process of, engaging Muslim women in community sport. The research focuses on how and why a community sport organization, located in a large Australian city, embraced cultural change and developed a more inclusive community sport environment through social capital facilitation. The operation of the three types of social capital (bonding, bridging and linking) is considered alongside social capital attributes (networks, trust, reciprocity, volunteering and community building). The theoretical framework employed is derived from Lin's framework of social capital. The research findings are analysed through an examination of the stages of investment, development, mobilization and reproduction of social capital. This research illustrates the potential for the development of trust, cooperation and community networks, leading to cultural awareness, and changes to the cultural profile and practices of community sport organizations.

A Culture of Trust: Engaging Muslim Women in Community Sport Organizations

Research indicates that many women from culturally and linguistically diverse backgrounds, including Muslim women, are proportionately less active in sport and recreation activities in Western countries than the corresponding generic female population (Cortis, Sawrikar, & Muir, 2007; Women's Sport and Fitness Foundation, 2009). A number of reasons have been put forward for this "under-representation", such as non-inclusive practices of sport organizations, restrictive community attitudes and values, lack of appropriate venues and/or opportunities that allow culturally appropriate clothing to be worn, and scarcity of female-only sporting environments (Hanlon & Coleman, 2006; Palmer, 2005; Sfeir, 1985; Walseth, 2006). Studies on this matter have also identified specific religious requirements that present challenges for Islamic immigrants residing in non-Islamic countries (Dagkas & Benn, 2006; DeKnop, Theeboom, Wittock, & DeMartelaer, 1996; Hargreaves, 2000; Kahan, 2003). However, it should be noted that Muslim women are not prohibited from activity by Islamic tenets (Kahan, 2003; Sfeir, 1985), with swimming, archery and horse-riding specifically encouraged.

In many countries, Muslim women participate in competitive sport and have demonstrated success and achievements at various levels of sport participation, including elite sporting competitions such as the Olympics (Kahan, 2003). Evidence suggests that Muslim women who regard religion as a source of identification often view physical activity positively (Walseth, 2006). Some Islamic countries provide their female population with a culturally complementary sport infrastructure that allows for sport participation to occur within culturally acceptable parameters (Sfeir, 1985). Such parameters may encompass women playing sport in female-only sport settings, or with adherence to a stipulated dress code (Women's Sport and Fitness Foundation, 2009). The lack of access to and provision of culturally inclusive sport environments in some Western countries, such as Australia, has been identified as a critical factor in Muslim women's lower participation rates and lack of viable opportunities to engage in sport and accrue the benefits of participation (Taylor, 2003).

In Australia, a country of just over 21 million, the 2006 census recorded over 340,000 Muslims (approximately one-third of this group was born in Australia), of which the largest countries of origin were Lebanon and Turkey. Although the 2006 census does not provide specific sports participation rates for Muslim women as a group, it shows a 19.7% regular participation rate for women originating in North Africa and the Middle East, compared to a participation rate of 66% for women born in Australia (Australian Bureau of Statistics, 2007). This indicates that women from the Middle East have a lower sports participation rate than those born in Australia. In juxtaposition, other research has found that amongst the Australian Muslim population there is an increasing desire for young Muslim women to participate in sport (Palmer, 2009).

In a wide-ranging investigation of sport participation of women from culturally and linguistically diverse backgrounds in Australia, Cortis et al. (2007) argued that community sport organizations are in a particularly good position to provide an environment that encourages sport participation and the social inclusion of Muslim women. They suggest that the achievement of social inclusion outcomes could be delivered through the social function of sport, relating to social integration and civic participation. It has also been argued that community sport can be used to construct women's individual and group identity and provide an avenue for Muslim women to become ambassadors for their community (Palmer, 2009). Taking these premises as a starting point, the research outlined in this paper explores the engagement of Muslim women in community sport organizations, with a focus on the development of social capital and the resultant cultural change in the profile and practices of a community sport organization (CSO).

Community Building, Social Capital and Sport

The community-building role of sport has been linked to the notion of social capital by many researchers (Arai & Pedlar, 2003; Auld, 2008; Blackshaw & Long, 2005; Coalter, 2007; Collins & Kay, 2003; Doherty & Misener, 2008; Jarvie, 2008; Nicholson and Hoye, 2008; Rojek, 2005; Seippel, 2006; Tonts, 2005). Sport can be a site where substantive social capital is created (Nicholson and Hoye, 2008) and, in turn, social capital can facilitate social policy development and active citizenship. Social capital is generally considered a multifaceted concept composed of a number of levels, types, dimensions, attributes, indicators, features or elements.

In considering the community development aspect of sport, the communitarian conceptualization of social capital focuses on sport for the "common good" (Jarvie, 2003). In particular, it emphasizes community trust, cooperation and mutuality attributes (Arai & Pedlar, 2003). This also equates social capital with cohesion through participation in local organizations, voluntary groups and associations (Woolcock & Narayan, 2000). The attributes of social and inter-ethnic trust, social networks, reciprocity and volunteering and community well-being are of particular relevance to community sport.

While generally viewed in a positive light, not all social capital generates positive or inclusive outcomes. Sport has also been found to generate negative social capital, which acts to exclude individuals or groups based on social, cultural and/or religious differences (Tonts, 2005). Sporting clubs' restrictions on individual freedoms, gender distinctions and discrimination, and downward levelling of norms, can all lead to exclusion or marginality of some groups (Coalter, 2007; Coffe & Geys, 2007; Jarvie, 2003; Portes & Landolt, 2000).

Nevertheless, it is argued here that sport has the potential to create positive social capital in the form of trust, openness and respect for different individuals and groups that may also facilitate greater cooperation and increase social cohesion within communities. To date, the literature has yet to fully categorize and empirically confirm the contribution that sport makes to the building of social capital. In order to contribute to an evidence base, the study reported in this paper specifically looks at whether involvement with a community sport organization (CSO), can provide a minority community group—Muslim women—with the opportunity to develop social capital, using the CSO as the unit of analysis. Previous studies examining sport and cultural diversity have justifiably been from the perspective of the individual or the community but, as our exploration of the issues expands, researchers can benefit from approaching the situation from different stakeholder perspectives.

In many multicultural countries sport organizations regard the inclusion of culturally defined minority groups as a critical consideration, one that has a direct impact on the sport's numbers of players, volunteers, spectators and employees, and essential to growth and sustainability of the organization (Taylor, 2003). Cultural inclusivity has demonstrated many positive outcomes for sport participants, the community and the organization involved (Cortis et al. 2007). In light of the considerations outlined above, the purpose of this study was to explore the social processes manifest in a community sport organization and how these might contribute to the development and operation of social capital for Muslim women. The next section presents a brief review of social capital theory and the theoretical framework used to inform the research.

Literature Review

Social Capital Underpinnings

In recent years there has been a heightened discussion of social capital and sport in academic and policy debates (Nicholson & Hoye, 2008; Tonts, 2005). Social capital as a concept has had a long history and is rooted in classic sociology; however, in more recent years social capital has been explored and popularized through the work of Bourdieu (1986), Coleman (1988), Lin (2001) and Putnam (2000). Putnam (2000, p. 19) described social capital as "connections amongst individuals—social networks". This social network conceptualization has been employed widely in academic research and debate. Portes and Landolt (2000) explain that social capital allows individuals to obtain benefits through memberships in networks and other structures of society. Their social capital definition has two components: (i) a relationship element that is embedded in the social organizations to which the individual belongs; and (ii) the relationship to the resources that the individual can claim by virtue of being a member in the group.

There are many definitional and conceptual interpretations within social capital literature (Blackshaw & Long, 2005); however, common ground for social capital theorists centres on the concept of social networks having value. The logic of the argument is that the better connected people are, the better off they will be emotionally, socially, physically and economically (Nicholson & Hoye, 2008). These connections between individuals were termed by Cox (1995) as the "social glue" that ties members of a given place to one another. The networks created through various forms of engagement in associated and civic activities that involve personal interaction, produce greater disposition towards trust and reciprocity (Mohan & Mohan, 2002). The understanding of social capital in this research context is thus considered to involve social relationships and the resources that are made available through these relationships.

As previously outlined, social capital is considered by scholars to be a complex multifaceted concept with a number of social capital types and attributes. Three types of social capital—bonding, bridging and linking—

have been identified by social capital theorists (Putnam, 2000; Woolcock, 2001). Nicholson and Hoye (2008, p. 7) refer to the work of Putnam, describing bridging social capital as the "processes by which the development of social norms, networks and trust through social interaction links various segments of the community and contributes to the connection of disparate elements of the community". Nicholson and Hoye (2008, p. 7) defined bonding social capital as "the norms, networks and trust contributing to the cooperation of members within a group" and highlighted that this can, in some cases, be exclusive rather than inclusive. The concept of linking social capital, as drawn from the work of Coalter (2007), is considered by Nicholson and Hoye (2008, p. 7) to be the "vertical connections between different social strata that enable individuals to gain access to other resources".

Social Capital in Community Sport Organizations

The view that the membership-based nature of CSOs can provide ideal sites for the creation of social capital has gained support in recent years (Auld, 2008; Hoye & Nicholson, 2009; Misener and Doherty, 2009; Seippel, 2006; Sharpe, 2006; Tonts, 2005). This notion of sport contributing to social capital has also gained support from government agencies in Australia, Canada and England (Hoye & Nicholson, 2009). Until recently very few empirical studies examined the development of social capital in specific institutional or organizational settings. Many of these studies, which generally focus on quantitative methods, have been undertaken in the last decade (Bradbury & Kay, 2008; Brown, 2008; Hylton, 2008; Long, 2008; Seippel, 2008) and are detailed in Nicholson and Hoye's (2008) *Sport and social capital*. Of particular relevance here is the work of Seippel (2008), which found that members of voluntary sport organizations in Norway developed social capital that was conducive to generalized trust and political commitment. Misener and Doherty's (2009) examination of a Canadian sports club concluded that the CSO they investigated had played an essential role in developing relationships and network capacity. Respect, trust and openness were found to be key factors in building relationships. All participants in their study viewed relationships with other organizations and stakeholders in the community to be beneficial for attaining required resources, whether human, technical or material.

The potential for social capital generation in CSOs is not always realized. Some evidence suggests that community sport organizations do not, to any great extent, develop the type of relationships necessary with their stakeholders to generate social capital (Allison, 2001; Barnes, Cousens, & MacLean, 2007; Cousens, Barnes, Stevens, Mallen, & Bradish, 2006). These research projects looked at organizational network contexts using social capital frameworks and did not find evidence that networks and trust developed sufficiently to produce social capital in the form of reciprocity or shared resources.

Social Capital Framework

The conceptualization of social capital employed in previous research on sports clubs has considered how the process of social capital production and reproduction can take place within CSOs through relationships and networks with others in the community (Doherty & Misener, 2008; Seippel, 2006; Sharpe, 2006). Researchers examining social capital in sport thus far have generally used frameworks that focus on a single aspect or element of social capital, such as trust (Seippel, 2006), volunteering (Auld, 2008; Bradbury & Kay, 2008) or networks (Doherty & Misener, 2008). These frameworks have been employed in sporting contexts more commonly at the micro- or macro-level and less frequently at the meso- or organizational level and, to date, social capital has not been empirically explored through multidimensional models.

As we sought to understand whether social capital processes were developed in the CSO environment and, if they were, how they developed and operated, we chose to take a different approach and examine social capital by drawing on the social capital model developed by Lin (2001). This framework operationalizes a social capital conceptualization which premises the notion of an investment in social relations with expected returns in the marketplace (Bourdieu, 1986; Portes & Landolt, 2000). This signifies that capital can be captured through social connections and social relations and capital is seen as a social asset. Furthermore, social capital is presented as critical to organizations in achieving their objectives and goals as it represents an aggregation of valued resources of members interacting as a network. Lin provides four explanations as to why embedded resources in networks will enhance outcomes. These include: facilitating the flow of information; exerting influence on agents; conceiving social ties as social credentials; and reinforcing identity and recognition through social connections. The processes of investment, access, mobilization and returns on social capital provide a context which reflects the complexities of social capital and assumes an initial investment in resources followed by phases where the resources are accessed, used and returns are made. Returns on social capital investments can be instrumental (economic, political or social) or expressive (physical health, mental health and life satisfaction). This perspective on social capital allowed us to examine the phases of cultural inclusion and change through an exploration of investment in social relations, utilization and development of social capital and social capital reproduction.

Lin's framework includes a three-stage model: (i) an inequality in investment in social capital stage (influenced by the availability of collective assets, social resources and mobilized social resources); (ii) an access and mobilization of social capital stage; and (iii) a returns on social capital stage. This three-stage model allows for the exploration of the operation and development of a multifaceted concept (including types and attributes) of social capital at the meso-/organizational level through a deployment of both structural (e.g. networks and interpersonal relationships) and cognitive elements (e.g. norms, trust and cooperation) of social capital. The three commonly differentiated types of social capital (bonding, bridging and linking), conceptualized by Putnam (2000) and Woolcock (2001), are included within each developmental stage as well as social capital attributes such as trust and reciprocity.

Method

Case-study research was used to explore the social capital processes operating within the CSO at the meso-level. A case study approach was appropriate for developing a contextual in-depth understanding of how a contemporary community sport organization can employ social capital processes to engage culturally diverse groups and, furthermore, case study provided a suitable context for the application of the Lin framework. Case-study inquiry fits well with this investigation as it relies on multiple sources of evidence (e.g. historical records, interviews and club documents) and it further benefits from the prior development of a theoretical framework (i.e. Lin, 2001) which guides data collection and analysis. A constructivist approach was employed based on the philosophy that reality is socially constructed through language and shared meaning (Guba & Lincoln, 2004; Patton, 2002). This was deemed apposite for this research as it examines the development of social processes influenced by cultural interpretations of the social world.

A case study approach allowed us to answer the research question, which called for an investigation into the role of social capital in facilitating the engagement of Muslim women in CSOs. The specific case study was selected purposefully to allow us to examine the development and operation of social capital in a CSO which actively sought to change its cultural profile in order to become more inclusive and more fully represent its local community.

The Case Study

A CSO is defined as a membership-based, not-for-profit organization established to provide members with opportunities to participate in and support organized sporting competitions (Taylor, 2003). For the purposes of this investigation a mainstream community sporting organization which had an established reputation for specifically addressing the needs of Muslim women was chosen in order to explore the specific stages of social capital development as proposed by Lin (2001). This provided an opportunity to track how the CSO had evolved to its current state of inclusive operations. The case selection followed discussions with key stakeholders and decision makers working in the area of Muslim women and sport. To become familiar with the case organization and its community we established a rapport with the potential research participants through a number of meetings and visits to advocacy and partner organizations in the local area.

For the purpose of this study Muslim women were defined as women and teenage girls who self-identified as belonging to the Islamic religion and included both women born overseas and in Australia. Muslim women were selected as the focus for this research as they are under-presented in sport participation and are an identifiable group that face a number of cultural and religious challenges to their participation in active recreation in non-Islamic countries, such as Australia, as discussed earlier in this paper. Sporting engagement in this context encompassed playing, facilitating and watching sport (Nicholson & Hoye, 2008).

The CSO chosen for the study is situated in the Canterbury local government area in South Western Sydney, New South Wales, Australia. Canterbury local government area has an Islamic population of 13.7% (Canterbury City Council, 2009), compared to the Australian average of 1.7% (Australian Bureau of Statistics, 2007). The percentage of the non-Australian-born population in this area is 46.9% (Canterbury City Council, 2009), compared to 22% for Australia as a whole (Australian Bureau of Statistics, 2007). This voluntary non-profit CSO has a culturally diverse membership, including members born in Vietnam, Greece, Italy, Indonesia, Lebanon and Australia, which in 2009 comprised 21% women and 79% men.

The vision of the CSO according to its mission statement is to promote participation in sport by addressing religious, ethnic and social barriers. The CSO provides opportunities for female and junior soccer, which are unavailable at the neighbouring community club that caters only for male soccer. The CSO has a long history, with over ninety years serving the community sporting needs of the local young people. Historically, the CSO has been dominated by an Anglo-Australian male membership which competed in soccer, cricket and martial arts. Over the last decade the CSO has changed dramatically, mirroring the changing demographics of the local area. The CSO has become ethnically diverse across its sporting programmes, with participants from a Vietnamese, Greek, Italian, Indonesian, Australian and Lebanese background and a small number of refugees from Sudan. The club has developed a strong community focus and provides affordable sporting activities by subsidizing costs to local community members, including disadvantaged groups.

Data Collection

We conducted the research between January and April 2009 after approval was granted by the university's ethics committee. Case-study research methods adopted included a range of qualitative techniques, comprising focus group interviews, in-depth interviews and document analysis. The individual and focus group interviews were undertaken with key stakeholders in the organization, including administrators, coaches and participants, as well as with key external partners and community advocacy organizations. Individual interviews were conducted with seven administrators, one coach, two participants, two partner organizations and two advocacy organizations. Two focus groups were also held, one with a group of five coaches and one with a group of six participants. Informants included both Muslims and non-Muslims, and male and females. The Muslim informants had an Arabic background and came from the Middle East region. A female interviewer facilitated all the sessions, as it was felt that this was important for the female participants to feel at ease.

Individual and group interviews were conducted using a loosely determined discussion list of issues, problems and questions that were drawn from the social capital literature. The interviews covered: (a) the processes of Muslim women's engagement; (b) development of relationships; (c) development of trust and cultural awareness; (d) cultural challenges to participation for Muslim women; and (e) development of reciprocity, community well-being and volunteering. The individual and focus group interviews were approached with flexibility using the process of open-ended questioning, as recommended by Barbour and Schostak (2006). The opportunity for individual perspectives to be voiced, and then for the group members to discuss and interpret the issues, was provided through focus group situations.

Organizational documents covering the period 2004–2009 were collected from the CSO, partner organizations and advocacy groups and from web-based searches. These were examined first for general evidence of social capital types (bonding, linking and bridging), social capital attributes and any negative aspects of social capital. For example, annual reports were scanned for evidence of club members working together on projects (bonding social capital), the club working with local community sponsors (bridging social capital) and club involvement in community and sport development projects funded by government agencies (linking social capital). This was an important initial element of contextualizing the case study as it allowed us to acknowledge the case's peculiarities, its history and future expectations (Stark & Torrance, 2006). The documents contained: contemporaneous media reporting (media releases and local and national newspaper articles for the 2004–2009 period) which represented public perception and attitudes towards the CSOs and towards Muslim women; internal documentation (project reports and annual reports for the 2004–2009 period) which documented ways in which the organization set priorities for its development and evaluation of strategic goals; and external documentation (government reports mentioning the CSO, partner organization minutes and organizational websites) which provided public sources of accountability and reflected the marketing of the CSO.

Data Analysis

The staged social capital model detailed in the social capital framework section of this paper was deployed as an analytical tool in order to interpret and evaluate the data. First, all interviews and focus groups were transcribed verbatim from audio recordings. Based on our interpretation of coding approaches developed by qualitative researchers (Miles & Huberman, 1994; Neuman, 2003; Patton, 2002; Yin, 2009), data were sorted and coded using the three-stage model. For example, a section of a transcript stated, "To maintain trust you have to adapt to what the community and players want and need. The community was not comfortable about the interaction between the young guys and girls so the club had to adapt and change, so they changed the training day". This section of the transcript was coded to an open code, "Trust between organization and community is shown". This was later coded to the axial code, "Stage 2 Access and mobilization of social capital". The text was also coded to the axial codes of "trust" and "community building".

Informant comments that reflected key concepts and themes associated with social capital development and operation were extracted from the interviews and focus groups, e.g. the development of volunteering and establishment of trust. These themes were then investigated further in the other secondary sources outlined above. Analysis of written documents assisted with detailing the culture of the organization and also identifying the values underlying organizational policies (Simons, 2009). Documents were used to cross-reference and corroborate, and augment evidence from the other sources (Yin, 2009). Established criteria for verifying authenticity, including methods of triangulation (such as member-checking of transcripts for verification and clarification) and the use of multiple data sources ensured clarity of meaning (Guba & Lincoln, 1989). The documents were particularly scrutinized for evidence or lack of evidence of social capital stages, types and attributes at work. We cross-checked information from one data source with another and compared responses from different types of informants.

Results

The case-study documentation and data collected were analysed within the context of the three-stage model (Lin, 2001) with respect to the CSO's inclusion of Muslim women and girls.

Stage 1—Inequality of Investment in Social Capital

From the late 1990s through to 2004 the club went through a period of membership decline, key volunteers resigned and it experienced financial difficulties and could not afford to replace uniforms or equipment. The club was almost disbanded and, at one stage, only three members were left on the club board. Evidence gathered indicated that the CSO during this period had few gender and/or culturally inclusive management policies or practices in place. Some non-Anglo members were involved in the club (e.g. as parents of Muslim boys); however, the inclusion of Muslim girls/women as sport participants was minimal. The Muslim parents were generally unsupportive of Muslim girls/women playing soccer at the club. There was one soccer team for girls in operation and the Muslim girls that played for the team were asked not to wear the Hijab (i.e. they were expected to assimilate in terms of their physical appearance).

During this period the Muslim women in the community generally did not feel they could trust the CSO with their daughters. Local Muslim women had little involvement with the CSO, a non-Muslim female administrator describes the situation with Muslim girls at the time,

> Their parents didn't really want them to play ... which was probably due to lack of communication on the club's side of things ... they were dealing with two cultures all the time and a lot of them found it frustrating (Organiser #7, personal interview, 11 March 2009).

General female participation across the club had reached a low point, with just five registered female members in 2004. The situation at the CSO at this time is described by a non-Muslim female board member:

> My daughter wanted to play soccer so I brought her down ... they didn't have a coach at the time so I put my hand up to take on the girl's side. That was the first girls' side back in 1999 ... the committee fell apart ... there were only three of us on the committee. We just kept the club going for the next four to five years. The club mainly fell apart due to personal differences with different parents (Organiser # 7, personal interview, 11 March 2009).

The particular challenge identified by this quote was the need for more volunteers from the wider community as the critical knowledge about the club was invested in a very small and declining number of people. Interview data also suggested that failure to account for the changing local community preferences and demographics resulted in the near collapse of the organization and in severe financial problems. Interviewees explained that the club at the time appeared to be internally focused and was trying to maintain historically successful programs and practices without due regard to the obsolescence of this approach within the changing community structure. Within the interview data and club, media and relevant government documents there is no mention of the club reaching out to the wider community (bridging social capital).

The 1990–2005 period is characterized by few volunteers, lack of culturally inclusive management practices, little trust between the organization and the local community and limited community links. Taken together these attributes are indicative of a CSO that was operating with a lack of collective assets and few social resources, particularly in relation to the potential engagement of females and especially Muslim women and girls.

Stage 2—Access and Mobilization of Social Capital

A change in leadership at the CSO occurred in 2005 and two local Muslim community leaders joined the board. The new leadership introduced a number of changes, such as new equipment, including new uniforms bought by new local sponsors and community partners. These changes assisted club recruitment and helped increase the number of young people from the local community joining the club as members. Interview and focus group data indicate that ties with the local community began to develop during this period. A Muslim man from the CSO board described this process, "We approached the Muslim Women Associations and told them we wanted to have women in our club . . . we developed contacts and relationships through community organizations, through the media, through Arabic radio and Arabic newspapers" (Organiser # 1, personal interview, 30 January 2009). The 2006 Annual report and media articles from this period provide evidence that links were developed with local schools, community health services, mosques, community advocacy groups, the local Council and local businesses. The Muslim community leaders who had joined the CSO board explained how they used their existing community networks to attract new members.

Interview participants outlined how trust developed between the CSO and the local Muslim community through a strategy of incremental change. Board members of the CSO initially actively recruited Muslim girls from families who already had boys participating in club sporting activities. Muslim parents that were interviewed reported that they felt able to trust the club with their daughters and were therefore willing to let them join the club. In the interviews, Muslim women noted that they began to feel comfortable and willing to help with club activities, such as running the canteen and sharing transport. Club members described how co-operation began to develop with sharing of resources and led to greater levels of involvement, as illustrated by a Muslim women's comment, "From the perspective of the women, they saw the other women getting involved, that made them want to come round and get themselves involved with their kids" (Organiser # 3, personal interview, 4 February 2009). Displays of co-operation and trust between participants, between participants and organizers, between the CSO and stakeholders, and between the CSO and advocacy organizations were described by several interviewees. A female Muslim participant noted, "We have a great relationship with our coach . . . it's easy to trust her" (Participant # 1, focus group interview, 19 January 2009).

Recognition of the need for inclusive practices and greater cultural and gender diversity prompted a greater level of co-operation between Muslims and non-Muslims and ensured that the CSO made some adaptations in order that Muslim women could participate more fully. Non-Muslim club members accepted that this shift was necessary for the club's survival and the club documents and interviews provided indications of the gradual building of inter-ethnic trust. For example, two former non-Muslim board members became involved in negotiations with the local soccer association so that Muslim women in the club could play wearing the Hijab. The Hijab became accepted as part of the soccer team uniform. Many of the women interviewed for this study explained that they needed to feel comfortable and relaxed in order to participate.

Another example of more inclusive engagement of the local diverse community is illustrated by a Muslim man who was a community stakeholder: "At the management level there are people coming from different backgrounds Muslim, Indonesian, Lebanese, Greek, Italian and other backgrounds" (Stakeholder #1, personal interview, 6 February 2009). Other indications of the club's adaptations which facilitated the greater cultural inclusion of Muslim women included the development of girl's/women's-only training sessions, the development of women leaders and coaches, and the selection of women as coaches for the girl's teams. The parents of the participants during individual interviews explained that they were particularly keen that the club provided this differentiation for their sons and daughters. Additionally, culturally appropriate food was introduced to the canteen, including Halal meat and consideration was extended to players during religious events, such as Ramadan.

The wide range of initiatives adopted by the CSO demonstrate how valuing alternative cultures became embedded in practice. These adaptations were accepted by the non-Muslim participants as important not only to increase participation and to respond to the changing demographics of the area but also as a form of respect of different cultural values. A non-Muslim women coach explained, "Cultural awareness is important to get new Muslim women on board. A confidence has to develop between new women and the club" (Coach # 1, personal interview, 9 March 2009). These adaptations were negotiated by both Muslim women and non-Muslims. They allowed both Muslim and non-Muslim women to comfortably participate in the club as players. A number of these local women who initially joined the club to play soccer subsequently became coaches, managers and board members to participate in the fuller life of the club. When noting the role of Muslim women in the club, the Muslim male president stated "we treat the women with utmost respect ... they need to feel that it is their club. They are not outsiders ... females are encouraged to play decision making roles in the club" (Organiser # 1, personal interview, 30 January 2009).

Interview and focus group participants described how local Muslim and non-Muslim women within the CSO took on numerous volunteer roles and became community role models. The cultural profile of the club began to significantly change at this time. Parents, friends and former participants volunteered to manage teams, helping with club administration, running the canteen and participating in first aid, coaching and referee training. Such activities are indications of the presence of bonding as well as bridging social capital. As illustrated by this Muslim woman's comment,

> The guys start to bond together ... people in the community see you ... hanging out together ... and ask about the club ... it's all interconnected. Most of the sponsors are local and they talk to people about the club (Participant # 6, focus group interview, 19 February 2009).

Evocations of mobilization of social capital were found in the use of local community contacts and contact resources. Other indications of the presence of bridging social capital included the increasing numbers of team sponsors from the local community, increases in referrals from community organizations and a growing presence at community functions. Evidence of increasing community involvement was illustrated by the number of soccer teams, which increased from nine in 2005 to 24 in 2009 and the number of female teams from one to three during the same period. According to CSO informants, media reports and community stakeholders, by 2008/9 social trust, commitment to common goals, co-operation which benefits others, community links and reciprocity were in operation across a range of levels within the CSO. Taken together, these criteria provide evidence indicating that the club was at stage 2 and was able to provide a vehicle for the development of social capital.

Stage 3—Returns on Social Capital

By 2009, a range of established partnerships were in operation with both government and non-government agencies (noted by interviewees, reported in media releases, outlined in the 2006 Annual Report and in local newspaper articles). These partnerships provided opportunities for the club to access external resources, specific activities, programmes and community events and to further engage women from the local community. Club members interviewed described these developing networks as a notable feature of the club. In the interviews and focus groups, partnerships were discussed in terms of developing trust and co-operation between the club and the wider community. These networks were demonstrated through club and individual participation in government-sponsored community development projects, such as activities organized to promote community harmony, sport development projects, community coaching initiatives and sport leadership courses. In the interviews, organizers noted that these networks had played a part in bringing in new resources, participants and skills into the organization. This indicated that instrumental returns were being made on initial investment in developing networks.

A Muslim woman who was a club organizer outlined the benefits of these networks, "We get more activities happening when we work with the Australian Sports Commission, they ran a few programmes that we were lucky enough to participate in" (Organiser # 4, personal interview, 19 January 2009). The value of partnerships and collaborations was frequently mentioned by interview and focus group participants. Partnership activities included participation in community events and festivals. Fundraising activities, working with partners in the local community, had become an important part of club activities, together with the attraction and servicing of sponsors and obtaining government grants. In interviews with club organizers, partner organizations were also noted for their understanding of the religious and cultural requirements of local women. This knowledge is of value to the CSO when recruiting and working with the local community.

Notions of volunteering and reciprocity were frequently mentioned in interviews, leading us to suggest that the club developed rich bonding social capital. Human resources were extended from three volunteers in 2004 to over 70 by 2009, according to the club annual reports. Managers and board members interviewed all discussed the importance of volunteering and giving back to the community by providing community service for young people by offering training support, opportunities to manage and coach teams, as well as providing gala and open days. Interviewees identified situations and practices that suggested strong bonding social capital amongst Muslim female participants within the CSO. These close ties or bonding social capital are not necessarily positive for everyone. An example of a non-Muslim women feeling excluded is outlined by a former team manager, "It's very focused on Islamic principles, way too much for a sports club. I'm not involved this year because religion is too heavily involved" (Coach # 2, personal interview, 9 March 2009). For this particular individual the CSO's focus has made her feel uncomfortable within the organization. The downside of making accommodations to engage Muslim women and stressing Islamic principles is that these moves may not be viewed as inclusive of other religious and cultural groups. However, evidence of the clubhouse being used both for Friday prayers and Sunday church services indicates that the CSO was attempting to act equitably.

Discussion

The results indicate a connectedness between the CSO-facilitated social capital development and the initiatives to change the cultural profile of the CSO from a relatively monoculture to a multicultural organization. Lin's (2001) three-stage social capital framework enabled us to look at this changing cultural profile over a six-year period (2004–2009) and, specifically, to investigate how the development and operation of social capital was connected to the engagement of Muslim women. The framework allowed us to go beyond an examination of social capital types and networks and enabled the development of a richer and deeper contextually-based understanding of social capital operation over time. It provided a staged structure to analyse the findings; none the less, we do accept that this model has limitations. Social capital attributes, such as trust and networks, may develop in an uneven manner which is not fully accounted for in a staged approach such as this, especially given their multifaceted and non-linear nature. The types of social capital do not always develop evenly. For example, in this case study, evidence of bonding social capital was apparent between some groups but not manifest across the whole CSO, as evidenced by a non-Muslim woman dropping out of the organization.

The staged approach has, however, provided a means of better understanding, interpreting and analysing the narrative of the CSO. The findings indicated, first, that within the CSO, co-operation, trust, networks and reciprocity were created through cultural accommodations, which reflected investment in social capital. This investment occurred through the development of trust and co-operation and the data suggest that the cultural perceptions of those within the CSO began to change as the organization attracted more multicultural members. This development of a culture of volunteering and reciprocity indicated that bonding social capital was also facilitating the process of cultural change within the CSO.

Secondly, the development of social networks through participation in local events, increased participation in CSO activities, and stakeholder initiatives reflected the access and capitalization phases of social capital development. We found that social capital in the CSO was being generated within inter-group relationships. The CSO created an environment that valued relationships and the club developed its network capacity accordingly and, furthermore, recognized relationships as an asset to the club. This development of community networks through bridging social capital facilitated the increasing participation of Muslim women in the CSO during this period.

Thirdly, the development of community partnerships and diverse community networks by the CSO demonstrated linking social capital in operation. This linking social capital in turn led to the reproduction of social connections through participation in leadership camps, coaching club teams and community coaching courses, resulting in claims of increases in life satisfaction and of improved skills and knowledge. Improved life skills, team-building experiences and community service opportunities support the proposition that sport can build community identity and a sense of community belonging (Tonts, 2005). These partnerships or linking social capital provided further opportunities for trust and community belonging to develop between individuals and different cultural groups within the CSO.

There was evidence that a CSO can build a relationship between sport and social capital development, as proposed by the literature (Nicholson & Hoye, 2008) and that this is demonstrated through the measures identified above, which included developing bridging and linking social capital, increasing levels of reciprocity and cultural adaptations that encourage cultural diversity and gender equity. However, adaptations to accommodate different perspectives should not erode the trust or co-operation of other religious or cultural groups within the organization. Other groups should feel included and be consulted on organizational initiatives so that they are not alienated by the process.

Overall, the development of cultural awareness within the CSO indicated that encouraging cultural diversity, through co-operative practices, was a factor in the engagement of a variety of religions and cultures within the organization. For example, the importance and benefits of accommodating a flexible uniform, which respects religious beliefs and at the same time preserves the collective identity of the team, was identified through this research. This finding is also supported by Palmer's (2009) study of young Muslim refugee women in South Australia. Through these practices the case study organization demonstrated that it respected religious modesty and accepted that women in the CSO had diverse veiling requirements according to their interpretations of Islam. These practical adaptations indicated that cultural difference had become recognized by the CSO and these differences had been accepted and club practices modified accordingly. The implications of this research for CSOs trying to change their cultural profile and become more culturally inclusive are that trust, co-operation and community building need to be developed through extending community networks and making adaptations to club practices so they are more culturally inclusive.

Concluding Remarks

Our findings lead to two main recommendations for future research and practice. First, we support the notion that CSOs are a potential site for the production and (re)production of social capital (Auld, 2008; Doherty & Misener, 2008) and, as such, they can be seen to value, respect and manage cultural diversity through developing approaches that assist groups such as Muslim women and thus actively promote cultural awareness and gender sensitivity. Secondly, CSOs are potential sites for the development of social capital with the possibility of providing opportunities for social cohesion and community development for Muslim women. Research investigating CSOs at different stages of maturity in terms of how they approach gender issues and cultural diversity would also further substantiate claims made in this paper about cultural change and changing cultural perceptions within CSOs and provide further supportive empirical evidence.

The unique and diverse cultural and religious requirements of Muslim women playing sport in Western countries should be openly acknowledged, further researched and better understood so that CSOs can engage, manage and involve Muslim women more fully, since they are often under-represented as sport participants, volunteers, coaches, officials and administrators. The value of developing cultural diversity within CSOs lies in breaking down participation barriers, creating opportunities by developing a sense of belonging and improving understanding within the organization itself which creates benefits for individuals, the organization and the wider community. This paper has provided some insights into the approaches that CSOs can employ to develop social capital (i.e. through developing trust, co-operation and community networks). This research has also demonstrated that by bridging, bonding and linking social capital the cultural profile and cultural practices of a CSO can be altered in order to meet the changing profile of the local community. Furthermore Lin' (2001) three-stage social capital framework provided a useful tool for an examination of the changing cultural profile of a community sport organization.

References

Allison, M. (2001). *Sports clubs in Scotland*. Edinburgh, UK: SportScotland.

Arai, S., & Pedlar, A. (2003). Moving beyond individualism in leisure theory: A critical analysis of concepts of community and social engagement. *Leisure Studies*, *22*(3), 185–202.

Auld, C. (2008). Voluntary sport clubs: The potential for the development of social capital. In M. Nicholson, & R. Hoye (Eds.), *Sport and social capital* (pp. 143–164). Oxford, UK: Butterworth-Heinemann.

Australian Bureau of Statistics. (2007). *Australian basic community profile 2006*. Census Community Profile Series, Cat No 2001.0, Canberra: Australian Bureau of Statistics.

Barbour, R.S., & Schostak, J. (2006). Interviewing and focus groups. In B. Somekh, & C. Lewin (Eds.), *Research methods in the social sciences* (pp. 41–48). Newbury Park, CA: Sage.

Barnes, M., Cousens, L., & MacLean, J. (2007). From silos to synergies: A network perspective of the Canadian sport system. *International Journal of Sport Management and Marketing*, *2*(5/6), 555–571.

Blackshaw, T., & Long, J. (2005). What's the big idea? A critical exploration of the concept of social capital and its incorporation into leisure policy discourse. *Leisure Studies*, *24*(3), 239–258.

Bourdieu, P. (1986). The forms of capital. In J. Richards (Ed.), *Handbook of theory and research for the sociology of education* (pp. 241–258). New York: Greenwood Press.

Bradbury, S., & Kay, T. (2008). Stepping into community? The impact of youth sport volunteering on young people's social capital. In M. Nicholson, & R. Hoye (Eds.), *Sport and social capital* (pp. 285–315). Oxford, UK: Butterworth-Heinemann.

Brown, K. (2008). Community sport/recreation members and social capital measures in Sweden and Australia. In M. Nicholson, & R. Hoye (Eds.), *Sport and social capital* (pp. 165–186). Oxford, UK: Butterworth-Heinemann.

Canterbury City Council. (2009). Demographics-and-interesting-statistics. Retrieved November 17, 2009, from http://profile.id.com.au/Default.aspx?id=147&pg=106&gid=10&type=enum.

Coalter, F. (2007). *A wider social role for sport: Who's keeping the score?*. Abingdon, UK: Routledge.

Coffe, H., & Geys, B. (2007). Toward an empirical characterisation of bridging and bonding social capital. *Nonprofit and Voluntary Sector Quarterly*, *36*(1), 121–139.

Coleman, J.S. (1988). Social capital in the creation of human capital. *American Journal of Sociology*, *94*(Suppl.), 95–120.

Collins, M., & Kay, T. (2003). *Sport and social exclusion*. London, UK: Routledge.

Cortis, N., Sawrikar, P., & Muir, K. (2007). *Participation in sport and recreation by culturally and linguistically diverse women*. Discussion Paper. Report for the Australian Government Office for Women, SPRC Report 4/07, University of New South Wales.

Cousens, L., Barnes, M., Stevens, J., Mallen, C., & Bradish, C. (2006). Who's your partner? Who's your ally? Exploring the characteristics of public, private, and voluntary recreation linkages. *Journal of Park and Recreation Administration*, *24*(1), 32–55.

Cox, E. (1995). *A truly civil society*. Sydney, Australia: ABC Books.

Dagkas, S., & Benn, T. (2006). Young Muslim women's experiences of Islam and physical education in Greece and Britain: A comparative study. *Sport, Education and Society*, *11*(1), 21–38.

DeKnop, R., Theeboom, M., Wittock, H., & DeMartelaer, K. (1996). Implications of Islam on Muslim girls' sport participation in Western Europe: Literature review and policy recommendations for sport and promotion. *Sport, Education and Society*, *1*, 147–164.

Doherty, A., & Misener, K. (2008). Community sport networks. In M. Nicholson, & R. Hoye (Eds.), *Sport and social capital* (pp. 113–142). Oxford, UK: Butterworth-Heinemann.

Guba, E.G., & Lincoln, Y.S. (1989). *Fourth generation evaluation*. Newbury Park, CA: Sage.

Guba, E.G., & Lincoln, Y.S. (2004). Competing paradigms in qualitative research. In S. W. Hesse-Biber, & P. Leavy (Eds.), *Approaches to qualitative research: A reader on theory and practice* (pp. 17–38). New York: Oxford University Press.

Hanlon, C., & Coleman, D. (2006). Recruitment and retention of culturally diverse people by sport and active recreation clubs. *Managing Leisure*, *11*(2), 77–95.

Hargreaves, J. (2000). *Heroines of sport: The politics of difference and identity*. London, UK: Routledge.

Hoye, R., & Nicholson, M. (2009). Social capital and sport policies in Australia. *Public Management Review*, *11*(4), 441–460.

Hylton, K. (2008). Race equality and sport networks: Social capital links. In M. Nicholson, & R. Hoye (Eds.), *Sport and social capital* (pp. 257–283). Oxford, UK: Butterworth-Heinemann.

Jarvie, G. (2003). Communitarism, sport and social capital. *International Review for the Sociology of Sport*, *38*, 139–153.

Jarvie, G. (2008). Narrowing the gap through sport, education and social capital? In N. Nicholson, & R. Hoye (Eds.), *Sport and social capital* (pp. 93–109). Oxford, UK: Butterworth-Heinemann.

Kahan, D. (2003). Islam and physical activity: Implications for American sport and physical educators. *Journal of Physical Education, Recreation and Dance*, *74*(3), 48–54.

Lin, N. (2001). *Social capital: A theory of social structure & action*. NY: Cambridge University Press.

Long, J. (2008). Sport's ambiguous relationship with social capital: The contribution of national governing bodies of sport. In M. Nicholson, & R. Hoye (Eds.), *Sport and social capital* (pp. 207–232). Oxford, UK: Butterworth-Heinemann.

Miles, M.B., & Huberman, M.A. (1994). *Qualitative data analysis* (2nd ed.). London: Sage.

Misener, K., & Doherty, A. (2009). A case study of organizational capacity in nonprofit community sport. *Journal of Sport Management*, *23*, 457–482.

Mohan, G., & Mohan, J. (2002). Placing social capital. *Progress in Human Geography*, *26*, 191–210.

Neuman, W.L. (2003). *Social research methods: Qualitative and quantitative approaches* (5th ed.). Boston: Pearson Education.

Nicholson, M., & Hoye, R. (2008). *Sport and social capital*. Oxford, UK: Butterworth-Heinemann.

Palmer, C. (2005). *A world of fine difference: Sport and newly arrived young refugee women in Adelaide*. Study presented to Department of Gender Studies, University of Otago, New Zealand, September.

Palmer, C. (2009). Soccer and the politics of identity for young Muslim refugee women in South Australia. *Soccer & Society*, *10*(1), 27–38.

Patton, M.Q. (2002). *Qualitative evaluation and research methods* (3rd ed.). Thousand Oaks, CA: Sage.

Portes, A., & Landolt, P. (2000). Social capital: Promises and pitfalls of its role in development. *Journal of Latin American Studies*, *32*, 529–547.

Putnam, R.D. (2000). *Bowling alone: The collapse and revival of the American community*. New York City: Simon and Schuster.

Rojek, C. (2005). *Leisure theory: Principles and practice*. Basingstoke, UK: Palgrave Macmillan.

Seippel, O. (2006). Sport and social capital. *Acta Sociologica*, *49*(2), 169–183.

Seippel, O. (2008). Public policies, social capital and voluntary sport. In M. Nicholson, & R. Hoye (Eds.), *Sport and social capital* (pp. 233–256). Oxford, UK: Butterworth-Heinemann.

Sfeir, L. (1985). The status of Muslim women in sport: Conflict between cultural tradition and modernization. *International Review for the Sociology of Sport*, *20*(4), 283–306.

Sharpe, E.K. (2006). Resources at the grassroots of recreation: Organizational capacity and quality of experience in a community sport organization. *Leisure Sciences*, *28*, 385–401.

Simons, H. (2009). *Case study research in practice*. Los Angeles: Sage.

Stark, S., & Torrance, H. (2006). Case study. In B. Somekh, & C. Lewin (Eds.), *Research methods in the social sciences* (pp. 33–40). Thousand Oaks, CA: Sage.

Taylor, T. (2003). Diversity management in a multi-cultural society: An exploratory study of cultural diversity and team sport in Australia. *Annals of Leisure Research*, *6*(2), 168–188.

Tonts, M. (2005). Competitive sport and social capital in rural Australia. *Journal of Rural Studies*, *21*(2), 137–149.

Walseth, K. (2006). Young Muslim women and sport: The impact of identity work. *Leisure Studies*, *25*(1), 75–94.

Women's Sport and Fitness Foundation. (2009). Muslim women in sport. Retrieved November 17, 2009, from http://www.wsff.org.uk/documents/Muslim women in sport.pdf.

Woolcock, M. (2001). The place of social capital in understanding social and economic outcomes. *Canadian Journal of Policy Research*, *2*(1), 11–17.

Woolcock, M., & Narayan, D. (2000). Social capital: Implications for development theory, research and policy. *The World Bank Research Observer*, *15*, 225–245.

Yin, R.K. (2009). *Case study research: Design and methods* (4th ed.). Los Angeles: Sage.

Meanings and Functions in Olympic Consumption: A Study of the Athens 2004 Olympic Licensed Products

ARTEMISIA APOSTOLOPOULOU*, DIMITRA PAPADIMITRIOU**, & VASIA DAMTSIOU†

**Sport Management, School of Business, Robert Morris University, PA, USA; **Department of Business Management, University of Patras, Rio, Greece & †Technical Educational Institute of Patras, Greece

ABSTRACT This is an exploratory study of the meanings and functions of one aspect of Olympic consumption, the purchase of Olympic licensed products. More specifically, the present study attempted to examine the value Olympic licensed items hold for their owners by uncovering the meanings attached to those items. Using the Athens 2004 Summer Olympic Games as the setting, 280 consumers responded to questions regarding their reasons for purchasing Olympic licensed products as well as how they intended to use those products. Furthermore, an effort was made to assess what those products meant for their owners. The findings of this study point to the highly symbolic meanings embedded in the consumption of Olympic licensed products. The symbolic meanings revealed centered around three main themes: the Olympic Movement, national identity, and national political history and achievement. To a lesser extent, experiential and functional meanings attached to Olympic licensed items were also identified.

Introduction

Licensing has been defined as "a contractual method of developing and exploiting intellectual property by transferring rights of use to third parties without the transfer of ownership" (Mullin, Hardy, & Sutton, 2000, p. 140). Figures from the U.S. sport industry indicate that for the four major professional sport leagues licensing constitutes a significant revenue stream, with retail sales in 2007 reaching $3.3 billion for Major League Baseball, $3.25 billion for the National Football League, $2.05 billion for the National Basketball Association and $800 million for the National Hockey League (Sports Business Resource Guide & Fact Book, 2009).

According to Mullin et al. (2000, p. 141), licensing works because team licensed products allow fans to "take home" an otherwise intangible sport product. Licensed products can provide avenues for fans to express their support to a team and connect with other fans and can serve as memorabilia that preserve memories. And even though licensing has become an important marketing tool capable of delivering both tangible and intangible benefits to sport organizations, past research has placed limited attention on examining sport licensed items as sources of symbolic or experiential meanings for those who own and display them. From a methodological standpoint, the majority of studies have used professional or collegiate teams as context. However, sport licensing is prevalent in the sport event sector also where due to some events' uniqueness and sparse occurrence even deeper meanings and value could be attached to those licensed items.

Using the world's largest sporting event, the Olympic Games, as setting, the present study focuses on consumers' purchase of Olympic licensed items and the meanings those items hold for their owners. More specifically, the primary purpose of this research was to explore the meanings people attach to licensed items they purchased during the 2004 Athens Olympic Games. Based on symbolic interactionism, a few authors (Elliott, 1997; Solomon, 1983) contend that what a purchase means to the consumer depends on the consumption context in which one acts and the dominant cultural production system. During the four-year preparation for the Olympic Games, various cultural symbols are widely promoted, mainly at a national level, and new ones are generated and disseminated, creating a particular fertile ground for exploring meanings attached to Olympic licensed merchandise. The motivation driving consumers' buying behavior is another key area of research addressing why consumers purchase products and what benefits they seek from their consumption. The intended use of a product might actually influence what that product means for a consumer (Ligas, 2000). Therefore, the secondary purpose of our study was to identify the reasons that led consumers to their purchases of Olympic licensed items as well as the ways in which they planned to use those items.

The rarity of the Olympic Games as an event, the range and size of the audience it attracts, as well as the unique values tied to the Olympic brand, make the Olympic licensing program a great platform for conducting research that not only expands our conceptual understanding of sport licensing, but also provides insight on how to promote and to use licensing programs to generate favorable and unique brand associations.

Olympic Licensing

Licensing has become a fixture and a significant revenue source of the Olympic Movement through the sale of a variety of Olympic products as well as the sale of Olympic coins (numismatic program) and stamps (philatelic program). The Olympic licensing programs are managed by the Organizing Committees of the Olympic Games (OCOGs) and overseen by the International Olympic Committee (IOC) (Olympic Marketing Fact File, 2010). In the 2000 Olympic Games there were 100 licensees whose programs generated $52 million for Sydney's OCOG. In the 2004 Athens Games there were 23 licensees that generated $61.5 million in licensing revenues. Both of these figures were surpassed by the 2008 Beijing Olympic Games, during which period the licensing programs of 68 licensees made available 8,000 items in 1,000 retail locations, resulting in $163 million in licensing revenues (Olympic Marketing Fact File, 2010).

Central to the Olympic licensing programs are the well-publicized Olympic symbols: the five rings, the Olympic motto and creed, and the Olympic flame. As stated in a report generated by the Olympic Museum, "The meaning and the values of Olympism are conveyed by symbols" (The Olympic Symbols, 2007, p. 2). And those values are powerful, promoting *excellence* in athletic competition and in life; *friendship* despite their differences amongst the people of the world; and *respect* without discrimination across the five continents (The Olympic Symbols, 2007). The Olympic licensing programs are designed to promote the Olympic brand and to strengthen its image, while at the same time highlighting unique aspects of the host country's culture (Olympic Marketing Fact File, 2010).

Review of Literature

Consumption of Sport Licensed Products

Despite its widespread presence and also its significant bottom-line impact, sport licensing has surprisingly not received extensive attention as a topic of research. Most of the earlier research was part of larger studies dealing with the issues of sport consumer behavior (e.g. Fink, Trail, & Anderson, 2002; Wann, 2002), fan identification, involvement, and loyalty (e.g. Funk & Pastore, 2000; Kwon, Trail, & Anderson, 2006), and brand equity (e.g. Gladden & Funk, 2001; Gladden, Milne, & Sutton, 1998; Ross, 2006). It is posited that fans of a team will customarily engage in the purchase and display of items bearing the team name and logo (e.g. Fink et al., 2002), especially if those fans exhibit high levels of identification (Wann & Branscombe, 1993).

More recently, the study of sport licensing has been more focused and direct. Kwon and Armstrong (2006) looked at the impulse-buying tendencies of college students regarding athletic licensed products and attributed that behavior to students' identification with and psychological attachment to their university team. Subsequent work has shown that one's perception of value of the actual licensed items (Kwon, Trail, & James, 2007) and also a consumer's perceived value of the manufacturer-licensee (Kwon, Kim, & Mondello, 2008) significantly impact their intention to buy sport licensed products.

One gap that exists in the literature involves licensing of sporting events. The fact that some events occur only once or every few years, or only once at a particular location, adds more layers not only to consumers' purchase behavior but also to the value that those products might possess. With events, the window of opportunity to purchase a licensed item is much narrower than with team licensed items, a factor that may add to the urgency, even excitement associated with that purchase. Variables such as the scarcity of the event, its geographic and national scope, the socio-culture context of the host location, the distinctive values underpinning the event, availability and distribution of licensed products, and pricing have to be examined in order to obtain a more holistic understanding of the buying of licensed products.

Consumption of Product Symbolism

Although consumer behavior is a complex process, researchers agree that products are consumed not only because of their tangible attributes but also their intangible benefits. Individuals use products to satisfy particular functional needs but also to consume symbolic meanings, which are embedded in those products' image (Elliott, 1997; Fournier, 1998). According to Douglas and Isherwood (1996), products are part of a "live information system", which can be used by consumers in different ways depending on their needs.

In the marketing literature, the role of products as carriers of symbolism has emerged as an important topic for theoretical discussion and empirical research (Holt, 1995; McCracken, 1986). Richins (1994) distinguishes between the private and public symbolic meaning of products. This distinction accords with McCracken (1986) who suggests that products represent "displaced ideals" that can be either personal or social. Meanings are constantly grown within the culturally constituted world and pass to consumer goods through typical marketing tools, while subsequent consumption of goods signifies that those meanings pass from goods to consumers (McCracken, 1986).

The use of products as "commodity signs" has been extensively explored in the consumer behavior literature. Findings indicate that people purchase and use products to encode messages to others and decode messages from others (Elliott 1997; Solomon, 1983); to communicate an affiliation to a social group (Holt, 1995); to signify social status (Bourdieu, 1984); and as a means of self-expression, role playing, role fulfillment and judging others (Piacentini & Mailer, 2004; Solomon, 1983). In contrast, limited attention has been drawn to the role of mega-events, as a complex commodity, in building new markets and constructing new consumer identities. One exception is the published work by Maguire, Barnard, Butler, and Golding (2008) discussing extensively how the values underpinning Olympism have being repackaged into the "*Celebrate Humanity*" campaign, with the ultimate purpose of opening up new markets for IOC. Other relevant works have explored how international events, such as Euro'96 (Maguire & Poulton, 1999) and Soccer 2010 (Sewpaul, 2009), present a suitable platform for enhancing or reconstructing national identity, reestablishing national pride, repudiating stereotypes for nations, unifying/deconstructing nations and uniting or further dividing entities like Europe.

The socially constructed meanings of products are nurtured through the socialization process where consumers are exposed to meanings of symbols and engage in symbolic interpretation (Elliott & Wattanasuwan, 1998). Individuals make use of consumption symbolism by creating individualized product meanings through combining information in the marketing environment with their own "... personal goals, life history, context-specific interests, and the multitude of countervailing cultural meanings ..." (Thompson & Haytko, 1997, p. 16). Nevertheless, all scholars agree that product symbolism is not static and absolute, not only because products possess different meanings depending on the consumer and the intended use (Ligas, 2000; Solomon, 1983), but also because the particular meanings are constructed in a social environment that has the tendency to constantly negotiate the acceptance or rejection of these meanings (Ligas & Cotte, 1999; McCracken, 1986). The rationale for this assertion lies in the symbolic interactionism theory, which calls on a number of perspectives to justify the complex interplay among product social meanings, personal meanings and use intention (Blumer, 1969). From a more refreshed theoretical view, Arnould and Thompson (2005, p. 868) offer the term "Consumer Culture Theory" to capture the dynamic relationships among culture meanings, markets and consumer behaviors.

The theories discussed above are relevant to the context of Olympic licensed products and, given the exploratory nature of this research, will be used as points of reference for our data analysis. Olympic licensed products are primarily meaning-carrying goods with symbolism related to the Olympic Games and the Olympic Movement. Ligas' (2000) proposed product meaning categories, *functional* and *symbolic*, are used to analyze the emerging meanings associated with the consumption of Olympic licensed products. Unlike other approaches (e.g. McCracken, 1986), this scheme was chosen because it is based on empirical work and provides space for accommodating more abstract notions reflecting various conceptualizations of product meanings. Ligas' classification has been complemented with the *experiential* aspects of consumption underlined by Holbrook and Hirschman (1982, p. 134), which explore "the symbolic meanings of more subjective characteristics" of consumption (i.e. related to feelings and fantasies). McCracken's (1986, p. 71) framework for product usage also appears to be relevant to this work, not only because it brings to the forefront the notion that meanings are culturally constituted and "constantly in transit", but also because it suggests particular rituals, which denote how individuals consume conceptualized meanings attached to products.

"Athens 2004" as a Source of Meaning

Given that this research has set to understand consumer behavior related to the "Athens 2004" licensed products, it is useful to contextualize the particular Games by exploring (a) the social control processes following the preparation and the hosting period of this hallmark event and (b) the notion of Greek national identity and its possible influence on product meanings.

Throughout Olympic history, once nations are assigned the hosting of the Olympic Games they work consistently on social control to develop feelings of nationalism, community and pride. This is considered an integral part of the preparation for the Games; the spread of the Olympic spirit and the cultural legacy of the host nation. In the case of Athens 2004, the selling of the Games to the Greeks appeared to be an easy task as culture and history are at the base of Greek national pride. The Athens Organizing Committee (ATHOC) did not have to launch a global or national search for their slogan, but had to simply build on the long-standing relationship between the Olympic Games and national pride. The slogan "*Welcome Home*" was picked easily to convey not only a warm invitation to all members of the Olympic family, but also the joy and honor of having the Games back in their historical (and modern) birthplace. The nationalism of a historical Greek nation was also vividly present in the Olympic mascots, Athena and Phevos, and the Olympic logo, which featured an olive wreath in the national blue and white colors. Similarly, other slogans, such as "*In the true spirit of the Games*", "*Athens embraces the world*", "*Our flame unites the world*", "*Join us*" and "*Show them the Athens you love*", sought to sell the uniqueness of the Athens Games as the only and ever authentic and perhaps capable of transforming the symbolic landscape of the over-commercialized and commodified Olympic Games.

Also, social control was implicitly exercised by the promotion of the typical benefits of the Games, including the improvement of the Athens urban infrastructure, the development of sports infrastructure and the investment in the national tourism product. All of those much needed projects were, with the prospect of the Olympic Games, assigned a definite deadline.

However, equally as important was the government's and ATHOC's control over the planning and execution of the sport venue development and of security—issues emerging as particularly problematic in the case of the Athens Games. Nearing the Games, the venue development delays created tremendous concerns among the public about the ability of this small nation to carry successfully such a huge and expensive undertaking. Additionally, security concerns surrounding the first Olympics to take place after the 9/11 terrorist attacks did not simply raise the security budget to five times the equivalent of the Sydney Games, but also placed doubt on the credibility of the country in security issues. Both issues, by dominating the media, functioned as another strong mechanism for rekindling particular feelings of optimism, togetherness, eagerness for achievement and social responsibility. In this context, sport was once more transformed into a significant platform by which the nation became more "real" and the Games themselves turned to "patriot games" (Tuck, 2003) and were inevitably linked to national identity politics.

National Identity as a Source of Meaning

In Greece the discourse of national identity is associated not only with the modern nation-building process, which started in 1830, but also with the historical uniqueness of the Greek glorious antiquity that penetrates modern Greek identity. As Tsoukalas (1999, p. 8) put it, Greece is one of the rare and exceptional cases in the world where "... it is not the nations that built and reconstructed their pre-modern histories, but the pre-modern histories that develop into nation". The immense importance of the pre-national, pre-modern Hellenic civilization, along with the vast collection of monuments, ruins and narratives, imposed themselves on a modern state-nation with a strong but complex national identity. The Olympic Games and ideals constitute a unique part of this national identity as the most significant part of the ancient and modern Games' history and ideals has left indelible marks in the Greek land (i.e. Olympia, Panathinaiko Stadium, Olympic Flame Ceremony, etc.), culture and education. This largely explains the high level of nationalism, national pride and patriotism of the Greek population and the constancy on bidding and hosting the Games.

The Games indirectly concurred with other identity narratives derived from the glory of Greek antiquity, such as culture, social values, democracy, drama, philosophy, and presented an invaluable opportunity to be revived in a unique sport context. Moreover, as Hogan (2003, p. 103) states, "The modern Olympic Games ... exemplify tensions between globalism and localism and provide fertile ground for articulations of national identity". The present empirical study draws on previous findings and classifications of discursive themes by Maguire and Poulton (1999) in relation to national identity, sport and the media and by de Cillia, Reisigl, and Wodak (1999) in relation to national identity in order to explore the meanings consumers attach to Olympic licensed products.

Methodology

Setting

As the organizing body of the 2004 Athens Olympics, ATHOC was in charge of all licensing operations for those Summer Games. The committee's efforts involved 23 different licensees (19 national and four international) that offered over 5,000 types of products in 29 product categories through 10,000 distribution outlets in Greece alone (Athens 2004 Olympics, 2004).

Data Collection

A questionnaire with both open- and closed-ended questions was used covering the following areas: (1) the 2004 Olympic licensed items purchased; (2) the reasons that led consumers to their purchases; (3) consumers' intended use of those Olympic products; and (4) the meanings of those products for the buyers. In addition, respondents were asked whether they had purchased other (non-Olympic) sport licensed products in the past. Finally, some demographic information was collected.

Data collection took place during August–September of 2004 at two high-traffic shopping centers authorized to sell authentic 2004 Olympic merchandise in the host city of Athens. A research assistant approached shoppers during their shopping and invited them to participate in the study. In most cases the questionnaire was administered by the research assistant who asked the questions and wrote down shoppers' responses. Research efforts returned 280 usable questionnaires.

Sample

Respondents were part of a convenience sample, as for convenience purposes no systematic sample selection process was followed. All study participants were shoppers of Olympic merchandise items. Fifty-seven percent of respondents were female and most fell between the ages of 16–25 years (36%) and 26–35 (34%). Three-quarters of the sample (75%) reported having gained or were working towards a college/university degree. The overwhelming majority of the sample (88%) included Greek citizens.

Questions were also asked to assess the general sport profile of study participants. Eighty percent of respondents considered themselves sport fans and 74% agreed that they exhibited at least moderate levels of sport participation. Furthermore, a quarter (25%) of the sample had at least moderate interest in sport, while 61% indicated that their interest in sport was high or extremely high. One interesting finding relates to respondents' past purchases of team licensed products. Analysis of data revealed that the majority of respondents (76%) had not purchased team licensed merchandise in the past; their behavior was uniquely attributed to this event.

Data Analysis

Responses to the first open-ended question (i.e. items purchased) were coded based on the existing licensed product categories, as published by ATHOC. Data from the other three open-ended questions were recorded, reviewed and content-analyzed in order to identify themes within which responses could be categorized. Themes were mainly inspired by the data but also informed by past literature (Hogan, 2003; Holbrook & Hirschman, 1982; Ligas, 2000; Maguire & Poulton, 1999; Tuck, 2003). Following that process, two researchers independently coded all responses. For the questions involving reasons for purchase and intended use of the Olympic licensed items, the two coders were in absolute agreement. For the question involving the symbolic meaning(s) of the purchased items, inter-coder reliability was just over 93%. Differences were discussed by the coders and resolved. For the closed-ended questions, descriptive statistics were calculated.

Results

Olympic Licensed Items Purchased

In order to gauge which of those products were most popular among shoppers, study participants were asked to list the items they had bought (Table 1). A total of 875 items were listed through this process. Thirty-five percent of respondents said they had bought 1–2 items, while over half of the sample (55%) listed 3–5 purchased items. Results indicated that the five most popular Olympic licensed product categories were pins (19% of all items listed); toys, especially the Olympic mascots (13%); sports-wear, t-shirts mostly (12%); key rings and magnetic decorative items (9%); and hats (9%).

Reasons for Purchase of Olympic Licensed Items

Another goal of this research was to explore the reasons that led consumers to their purchase of Olympic licensed products, so study participants were asked to list up to three reasons that led them to their purchase. A total of 375 responses were received, which were content-analyzed and coded based on the themes that emerged from the data (Table 2).

Results point to the fact that having something by which to remember the Games (43%) and the actual features and quality of the products (27%) were the two main reasons why shoppers bought those Olympic items. A third reason that drove participants to their purchases was the fact that the

Table 1. Olympic licensed items purchased by product category ($n = 875$)

Product category	No. of items	% of items listed
Pins	163	18.6
Toys	117	13.4
Sports-wear	107	12.2
Key rings and magnetic decorative items	82	9.4
Hats	78	8.9
Stationery	67	7.7
Bags and travel goods	59	6.7
Household porcelain and ceramics	48	5.5
Towels and bathrobes	44	5.0
Frames and photo albums	26	3.0
Shoes	13	1.5
Posters and greeting cards	13	1.5
Casual wear	12	1.4
Jewelry	10	1.1
Beachwear	10	1.1
Others (e.g. glassware, puzzles, toys, bedding, computer accessories)	26	3.0
Total	875	100

Note: Six product categories (polo shirts, children's clothing, leather goods, pyjamas and underwear, sunglasses, editions) were not mentioned by any respondent.

Table 2. Reasons for purchase of Olympic licensed items ($n = 375$)

Reason for purchase	Total (%)
To keep as memorabilia, remember the Games	42.7
Product features, uniqueness, likeability	26.9
To help get into the spirit of the Games, to be trendy	7.7
To offer as gift	5.9
Functional/practical use	5.1
To collect, trade, sell	4.5
To support the Olympic effort	3.2
Emotional, ideological, historical reason	2.4
Other reason	1.6
Total	100

Olympic items were trendy (i.e. bought, worn, used by all) and could assist them in getting into the spirit of the event (8%).

Intended Use of Purchased Olympic Items

In addition to asking about the reasons of their purchase, another goal was to gather information in terms of how shoppers intended to use those purchased items, shedding more light into their thought process and overall purchase behavior. A total of 371 responses were generated from that question.

Two main themes emerged from the data. Respondents primarily intended to use those products in their daily life (47%) or intended to use them as memorabilia (31%). Interestingly, some respondents specified that they were planning on using their purchases during the Games (that was particularly true for articles of clothing), but that they would store those items away after the Games to have as memorabilia. In addition to those two themes, a relatively high percentage of purchases were also planned to be offered as gifts (20%).

Meanings of Purchased Olympic Items

Study participants were asked to describe what the Olympic products they had bought meant to them. Responses generated were categorized as symbolic, experiential or functional meanings. Those responses coded as symbolic meanings were further analyzed and revealed the following three themes: Olympic Movement symbolism; national identity symbolism; and national political history and achievement symbolism. A description of each theme as well as representative quotes are presented in Table 3.

The responses of about one-third of the sample included more than one meaning, each of which was coded separately. As a result, a total of 367 statements were analyzed. More than half of those statements (52.6%) made reference to some aspect of the Olympic Movement, while 20.7% expressed sentiments regarding the experience and feelings that study participants had

Table 3. Meanings of Olympic licensed items ($n = 358$)

Theme	Description	Sample responses	Total (%)
Olympic Movement symbolism	Institutions, elements or symbols of the Olympic Movement. Athens 2004. Athleticism and Olympic athletes. The return of the Olympic Games to their home country.	"The true revival of the Olympic Games in the country in which they were born and as close as possible to their authentic meaning. Solidarity, amity and, most importantly, peace." "They remind me of the real meaning of the Games and they give me hope that it might still exist somewhere behind all these interests." "That when we want to, we can. We can hold Games, become friends, have peace. Even for a short while." "They have great value due to the rare chance of holding the Games [again] in Greece." "Games that return to their birthplace."	52.6
Experiential	Direct participation in the Olympic Games as a spectator or a volunteer. Celebration, euphoria, invented nostalgia. Feelings of national esteem, pride, prestige.	"Something to remind me of this unique experience that I will never live again. I can't explain it. It is a feeling. It is the moment that I was inside the stadium and was crying non-stop from joy!" "They symbolize an unforgettable experience as a volunteer and great emotion for this grand event that took place in our country." "A big celebration in which all of us participated ... It wasn't the actual Games as an event, but what we were experiencing outside of the Games, the joy." "The Games that we experienced, celebrated, became emotional over, cheered. It was 10 days of unity and amity." "National pride that we put on the best Games."	20.7

Table 3 (*Continued*)

Theme	Description	Sample responses	Total (%)
National identity symbolism	The country of Greece and the Greek nation. Greek history, values, character, including stereotypes. Antiquity and ancient Olympic ideals. Positive exposure of Greece.	"They have symbolic value for the country and for me personally, simply because I am Greek." "... They remind us of Greece and that's why we bought so many. If it were somewhere else we would buy just one souvenir, while now we bought many to have." "They are memorabilia that symbolize the Games in my country ... and for us who live abroad this event is of even greater importance." "They symbolize ... our history and our tradition that was revived for a short while." "... Greece's ability to complete the Games with great success even at the last minute." "The fortune to feel something that my ancestors felt when these Games would take place in Olympia." "... We became the center of the world even for a short while."	10.6
National political history and achievement symbolism	Hosting an important sporting event for the history and development of the country. Times of flourishing and prosperity. Times of difficulty and crisis. Accomplishment, pulling it all together, hosting successful Olympic Games. Political triumphs. Athletic success.	"It's an important event for Greece." "The significant event that took place in my country and the benefit for sport. Development and improvement." "It symbolizes our effort to successfully put on these Games." "Symbolic value since our country proved that it was justly awarded such a significant institution [event]." "The Games that were successful despite the accusations and the scandals and everyone's pessimism. Everything was beautiful." "Symbolic value in terms of the superiority of our country." "... The [athletic] successes we had that we did not	9.5

Table 3 (*Continued*)

Theme	Description	Sample responses	Total (%)
Functional	Uniqueness of Olympic licensed products. Specific product attributes and features. Use/offer as a gift.	"They were simply different from the usual ones. They will never be available again and I, too, wanted to buy some." "They have functional value." "... they are useful in my daily life ..." "... It is a good idea for a gift, original and different."	3.8
No meaning/other response	Olympic products held no particular meaning. Other meanings not captured in categories above.	"Nothing at all." "A commercial transaction. Which is exactly what the true meaning of the Olympic Games has become." "I believe the only benefit is for the companies, to earn money through sport." "Nothing. An opportunity for us collectors to deal with new objects."	2.7

developed toward the Olympic Games. To a lesser extent, respondents felt that the Olympic products they had bought symbolized some aspect of their national identity (10.6%) or the country's political history and/or achievement in organizing the Olympic Games (9.5%). Interestingly, only 3.8% of the responses indicated that these licensed items had some functional meaning for their owners, which points to the highly symbolic nature of these purchases.

Discussion

The present study set out to examine issues concerning the Olympic licensed items of the 2004 Athens Summer Olympic Games. This discussion is divided into two main sections: First we discuss the types of Olympic products study participants purchased, as well as consumers' motives and their intentions in using these products. In the second section we highlight the meanings consumers attached to the items they purchased. Practical recommendations are offered throughout the section.

Olympic Licensed Products: Motives for Purchase and Intended Use

The three most popular categories of Olympic items amongst study participants were pins, toys/mascots, and sportswear, such as t-shirts. The widespread popularity of Olympic mascots Athena and Phevos might explain the high sales of items, while the appeal of Olympic sportswear could be due to the fact that those items would allow consumers to publicly display their affinity for and support of the Olympic Games.

Regarding the reasons that led to those purchases, having an item that would remind consumers of the Olympic Games was revealed as the primary reason for which consumers invested in these purchases. Given the uniqueness of the Olympic Games as a sport and cultural event, it is not surprising that these consumers would want something *tangible* to remind them of their participation in a once-in-a-lifetime event. Past research has proposed using such items to extend sport consumers' experience beyond the core product (e.g. Apostolopoulou, 2002). This reasoning was even further highlighted in the responses of those who did not permanently live in Greece and who intended to take these items back to their country of residence as keepsake of the experience they had in Athens.

What also seemed to be important in consumers' decision to purchase Olympic merchandise were their quality and unique features—an encouraging fact, given the sport marketer's ability to control both. Past literature has highlighted the role that quality plays in how brand extensions are evaluated (e.g. Apostolopoulou, 2002; Dacin & Smith, 1994), while brand characteristics such as the logo or colors have the ability to generate favorable brand associations (e.g. Gladden et al., 1998). These findings suggest that great consideration should be given to the design and promotion of the branding elements (e.g. logo, secondary marks, mascot(s), slogan, etc.) of each Olympic Games. In addition, offering products that are viewed as appealing in terms of quality and style might invite more people to use these products after the conclusion of the event.

Finally, another theme that emerged was the role of the Olympic products in getting people excited about the event that was taking place in their home country. This reasoning was well captured in one respondent's statement that "Everyone was going around in those and it was pretty. It was like we were all wearing the same clothes". This finding is somewhat surprising because most people in the sample had never bought sport licensed products before and also because the practice of using sport licensed merchandise for casual wear is relatively uncommon within the Greek society. The explanation might be found in the feelings of national pride and national identity that were repeatedly articulated by respondents. From a marketing standpoint, these findings suggest that notions of collective identity and belonging, as well as norms of popular culture (i.e. being trendy), should be highlighted in the positioning and promotion of Olympic licensed merchandise.

The findings regarding consumers' reasons for purchasing Olympic items are further supported by responses received to the question of how consumers intended to use those items. In particular, a large percentage of respondents said that they would use the products they bought as memorabilia. However, that was not the predominant answer to this question. Almost half of study participants indicated that they intended to use the Olympic items in their daily lives. This finding is significant for a number of reasons: First, it highlights the utilitarian, functional aspects of these licensed products. Secondly, it suggests that a well-developed portfolio of brand extensions can help broaden a consumer's involvement with and investment in a sport property (e.g. team, the IOC) and strengthen the relationship between that property and the consumer. Thirdly, it further promotes the idea that Olympic licensed items could provide the platform for the Olympic Movement to remain present in people's lives beyond the Olympic Games. It is, therefore, important that in their promotional campaigns sport marketers incorporate not only the symbolic but also the functional aspects of licensed products and that they emphasize the various ways in which these products can be used—including the idea of offering a sport licensed item as a gift.

McCracken's (1986) discussion of ways in which consumer goods can be used also sheds light on the multidimensional nature of sport licensed items. He presents four types of rituals (exchange, possession, grooming and divestment) through which meanings can be transferred from goods to consumers. Our findings in terms of how consumers intended to use the Olympic products they bought correspond to at least two of those types of rituals: *exchange*, where consumers offer products as gifts with the intention of transferring the meanings of those products to the gift recipients; and *possession*, where consumers talk about and display their possessions in order to transfer meanings from those possessions to themselves. Interestingly, McCracken (1986, p. 79) also states that through the ritual of *possession* "consumers are able to use goods as markers of time, space, and occasion". This statement is very applicable in our case, given the uniqueness of the Olympic Games and consumers' intention to keep the Olympic licensed products they purchased as mementos. To a lesser extent, *grooming*, which involves cultivating products so that their meanings and qualities can show, might apply to consumer-collectors' purchase of Olympic items with the intention to exchange or sell them.

Olympic Licensed Products: Symbolic Meanings

Respondents provided a rich and multifaceted account illustrating the meanings related to Olympic item possession. The majority of those meanings are what Richins (1994) calls "public meanings", because they are part of a society's common knowledge developed as a result of advertising and enculturation experiences during the bidding and hosting period of the Games.

As expected, most respondents attached to the particular objects symbolic meanings primarily related to the Athens Olympic Games and to a lesser degree the Olympic Movement and the Olympic ideals. More specifically, consumers' symbolic meanings were centered on the unique aspects of the Athens Games, which mainly relate to their roots in Greek history and their return to their birthplace ("[These products symbolize] Games that return to their birthplace"). Similar meanings conveyed the Games' tremendous national significance that turned them into "patriot games" ("Games in our country"). These accounts clearly illustrate that consumers attach to their Olympic products meanings with semiotic elements of their national identity in a way commonly shared by the local and national community, and promote what Maguire and Poulton (1999) called perceived "special charisma" embodied in their views of their nations. This invaluable opportunity obtained additional significance due to the lack of any hope to host the Games again in this small country ("They have great value due to the rare chance of holding the Games [again] in Greece"). Also, by stressing the concept of "our" Games, these symbolic meanings implicitly carry a sense of temporary cultural discontinuity with respect to other nations.

Internalizing the messages of the powerful media representations of the Athens 2004 Games,[1] respondents not only saw the products as an extension of the Games, but also as a true revival of the spirit of the Games. This is reflected in a series of meaning illustrations of which the following extract is just one example: "The true revival of the Olympic Games in the country in which they were born and as close as possible to their authentic meaning. Solidarity, amity and, most importantly, peace". Interestingly, with few exceptions, symbolic meanings related to the idealistic rhetoric of Olympism, as implemented and promoted by the Olympic Movement, failed to reflect in the meanings consumers attached to the Olympic products and to the Games in general. The few accounts reflected either some trust to the pre-eminent international cultural movement to promote the true and eternal values of the Games ("That when we want to, we can. We can hold Games, become friends, have peace. Even for a short while"), or some nostalgia or skepticism for the major inconsistencies evident between the ideals and the actual realities and practices associated with the Olympic Games and the Olympic Movement ("They remind me of the real meaning of the Games and they give me hope that it might still exist somewhere behind all these interests").

For a considerable number of respondents, the particular products were items through which to reconstruct their national identity. Borrowing de Cillia et al.'s (1999) way of operationalizing the particular notion, respondents used those products to convey images about their country ("They remind me of Greece, which is wonderful"); to portray the consumer's nationality ("They have symbolic value for the country and for me personally, simply because I am Greek"); to remind the nation's "imaged charisma", unveiled from its unique history, and to revive the history and the culture of this country ("They symbolize ... our history and our tradition that was revived for a short while"); and to be used as a means to activate their national identity in different contexts, such as living abroad ("They symbolize Greece. For us living abroad it is very important that the Games returned to their home country"). Interestingly, a more careful reading of all relevant extracts did not reveal any destructive nationalism or xenophobia, but rather stressed pride in national identification. In the same vein, for a few consumers the acquired Olympic licensed products were visible symbols that awakened an emotional experience of Greek history related to the ancient Olympic Games ("The fortune to feel something that my ancestors felt when these Games would take place in Olympia").

The symbolic meanings of the acquired products also reflected stereotypes related to national identity and the way the Greek public sector operates. Those sentiments were framed in positive terms mainly, probably due to the success of the Games. These stereotypes centered on "imaged'tpdel communities" and the nation's "imagined charisma" articulated in one respondent's words, as follows: "... Greece's ability to complete the Games with great success even at the last minute". These statements imply stereotypes about the lack of timely planning and control practices, which necessitate last minute preparations for the Games. Admittedly, the tremendous organizational success of the Athens Olympics offered an excellent opportunity for national identity politics in repudiating stereotypical notions, created and reinforced mainly by global media coverage because of the delays and complexities during the preparation period. As such, borrowing Maguire and Poulton's (1999) wording, "Athens 2004" can be seen also as a seven-year long social control mechanism towards European integration, and the particular licensed products as convenient carriers of this symbolism.

Finally, the perceptions of how the success of the Athens 2004 Olympic Games was eventually translated to a political and national triumph were also recalled as symbolic meanings related to the Olympic licensed products. More often, respondents implicitly made reference to the triumph of the Games, which contributed to the construction of a common culture and to political achievement and triumph: "Symbolic value since our country proved that it was justly awarded such a significant institution [event]". These symbolic meanings are fully understood by making reference to the identity politics dominating the media discourse, underpinning the difficulties of the pre-Game period.

Overall these results reconfirm the association between national identity and the Olympics or other major international events, or sport in general, which has been widely acknowledged (Horak & Spitaler, 2003; Kersting, 2007) and documented in the findings of sociology-oriented researchers (Hogan, 2003; Maguire & Poulton, 1999; Sewpaul, 2009; Tuck, 2003).

Olympic Licensed Products: Experiential Meanings

This research uncovered that Olympic licensed products were also viewed as sources of meaning that appealed to consumers' emotions, signifying a shift toward what Holbrook and Hirschman (1982) have called "experiential consumption". Based on the evidence, consumption of the particular products was linked to extremely positive feelings of being able to become involved in a once-in-a-lifetime experience, which led some to experiencing extraordinary emotions while attending the Games ("Something to remind me of this unique experience that I will never live again. I can't explain it. It is a feeling. It is the moment that I was inside the stadium and was crying non-stop from joy!"); taking part as a volunteer ("They symbolize an unforgettable experience as a volunteer and great emotion for this grant event that took place in our country"); joining the unforgettable celebration ("They represent the great celebration I lived in August 2004"); and being filled with joy and entertainment in a unique sport and cultural context ("A commercial but, at the same time, a very enjoyable sport and cultural event").

A considerable number of respondents used the questions about the products' meaning to describe the good feelings encountered while taking part in the Olympic Games. Those feelings were illustrated as unprecedented joy and pleasure not necessarily linked directly to the Games but to the wider celebration they were experiencing as a deeply unified community ("A big celebration in which all of us participated ... It wasn't the actual Games as an event, but what we were experiencing outside of the Games, the joy"). Similarly, the particular products turned to highly expressive consumption items conveying unique emotions of national pride, esteem and satisfaction associated with the organizational success of the Athens Games ("National pride that we put on the best Games"). In accordance with Holbrook and Hirschman (1982), the above findings enrich and supplement the previously discussed symbolic meanings by offering a mixture of experience-oriented meanings attached to the consumption of licensed products.

Olympic Licensed Products: Functional Meanings

Even though symbolic meanings overpowered consumers' reaction to Olympic licensed products, there was still a small percentage of those who expressed functional meanings regarding the items they purchased. Consistent with sentiments about the uniqueness of the Olympic Games as an event and also the reality that they will probably not return to Greece in the immediate future, consumers acknowledged that the Athens 2004 licensed products were equally as unique and a one-time occurrence ("They were simply different from the usual ones. They will never be available again and I, too, wanted to buy some"). Other respondents focused on these products' value as a gift ("... It is a good idea for a gift, original and different") or the ability to use them to complete daily tasks ("... they are useful in my daily life ...").

It should be noted that the number of functional meanings revealed (3.8%) is substantially lower than the percentage of responses indicating shoppers' intention to use the Olympic products in their daily lives (47%). The difference in the two percentages highlights even further the fact that when it comes to the value of Olympic licensed products (and perhaps sport licensed items, in general) symbolic meanings are overwhelming. Nevertheless, that does not negate the reality that these products can also have utility in one's daily activities.

Olympic Licensed Products: Other Meanings

Lastly, for a very small number of consumers the acquisition of the particular products reflected a negative attitude toward the exploitative elements of the Olympic Games. Those respondents did not view the Olympic licensed items as means to satisfy needs or to promote the true spirit of the Games. On the contrary, they indicated that the particular products were a reflection of the high levels of commercialization and the commodification of the Olympic Games.

Conclusions

The primary focus of this research has been to explore the meanings that consumers derive through the acquisition of licensed products linked to the 2004 Athens Olympic Games. Inspired by the work of McCracken (1986) and Holbrook and Hirschman (1982), a first effort was made to capture the range of symbolic and experiential meanings associated with "Athens 2004" Olympic licensed items.

The main evidence presented in relation to Olympic licensed product meanings shows that the particular products are not consumed for their material utilities, but consumed primarily for their social-symbolic meanings. They represent an exemplification of what Elliott (1997) calls products as "commodity signs" that offer feelings, illusions and images to the prospective consumer. The part of the analysis pertinent to the symbolism embedded in the particular goods revealed a multifaceted social symbolic universe from which consumers draw on to construct their national identity; to rekindle a perceived "special charisma" embodied in the opportunity of their country to host the Olympic Games (Maguire & Poulton, 1999); to renew a sense of locality and ownership attached to the Olympic Games because of history; and to display their unique experience and emotional association to their so-called "own" Games, signifying temporary distance from the "others". This presents the manner by which sport product consumption becomes associated with national identity, politics and culture and symbolic meanings pass from goods to consumers (McCracken, 1986).

The findings also support the idea that the acquisition of products can be understood as a source of meanings that are constantly constructed and consumed not only in a specific sport context but also in a discursive social space—in this case that of the Olympic Games hosted in their historical birthplace, a small country characterized by a weak economy and relatively insignificant geopolitical status. Admittedly, "Athens 2004" provided a fertile ground for various identity narratives to flourish and concur with other narratives, all important in fostering positive sentiments of patriotism, national pride and individual self-esteem. Validating the assertions by Holbrook and Hirschman (1982) about the value of an experiential approach to consumption, the results of this study provide a representative account of feelings and emotions attached to the particular products due to their direct link to the Olympic Games. The consumption of the particular items became an opportunity for articulation of feelings such as joy, pleasure, sense of taking part, celebration, as well as re-establishing national pride and esteem. Interestingly, all of these feelings are clearly detached from any utilitarian function that these Olympic products may or may not possess. From a consumer behavior research standpoint, the findings build on knowledge about the role of product symbolism in helping consumers construct their social reality (e.g. Elliott, 1997; Solomon, 1983). The results showed also how consumers draw on the symbolic meanings of Olympic products to construct a "we identity" through their own interpretations of the constructed contemporary sport culture, the discursive identity politics and the national culture.

In closing, the present findings add to the ongoing sport licensing discussion by illustrating how licensed products, especially those of unique events such as the Olympic Games, can move beyond their functional roles to serve as vessels of rich and complex symbolic and experiential meanings. Studying consumers' motivation for buying sport licensed items and identifying private or public meanings that those possessions hold for their owners can provide valuable guidelines in the positioning and promotion of sport licensed products and sport brand extensions in general.

Limitations and Future Research

With this work we, by no means, claim to provide a coherent and workable framework for understanding and integrating the multifaceted nature of Olympic licensed products. There are at least two reasons that make that goal challenging: First, even though the Olympic Games are a deeply culturally embedded event, they are also an event subject to transformation as the Games travel from one host country to the next. Secondly, the Athens 2004 Olympic Games were a unique case due to the historical aspects of those Games as well as the culture and identity of the nation itself. This limitation notwithstanding, the present study is, to our knowledge, the first effort to explore the meanings embedded in the consumption of sport licensed products. Future research should focus on upcoming Olympic events and explore all aspects of consumption of those Games' licensed products.

Another challenge that we faced in our research was the lack of concrete theory exploring symbols and special emotions, such as national pride and developing national identity, in relation to the consumption of sport licensed merchandise. Even though the relationship between mega-events and national identity is well established in sport sociology literature, sport consumer behavior literature has not adequately dealt with exploring the location of cultural meanings in relation to sport and event licensing. As Crawford (2004, p. 137) notes, we need to work more on recognizing "... the complex and fluid ways sport (and sport related goods) are consumed and located in everyday social patterns". Therefore, we recommend that the particular discursive themes reflecting symbolic meanings, identified in the present study, be considered as an orienting classification in need of further research. Given the fact that Olympic licensed products seem to encompass particularly rich and salient symbolic meanings, they constitute fertile ground for further culturally oriented sport consumer behavior research.

The methodology employed to solicit meanings that consumers held about their Olympic possessions could be seen as another limitation of our study. Specifically, the data collection procedure might have hindered how in-depth consumers were able to go with their reflections and resulting responses. A different setting (e.g. focus group, in-depth interview) could encourage a more thorough reflection and the revelation of more and deeper meanings, and is strongly recommended for future research efforts. Also, the data collection process used might be the reason why more private meanings of Olympic licensed products were not revealed in this study.

Finally, the fact that the overwhelming majority of the sample was composed of Greeks living in Greece or abroad can be seen as a limitation. Not surprisingly, sentiments of national pride and support for the home-host country as well as references to Greek history were widespread in the responses received. Including an equal number of non-Greek consumers could have potentially resulted in different themes about what the Olympic licensed products symbolized for their owners. Along with nationality, future research should also explore whether differences in views exist between consumers of different demographic make-up (e.g. age, socio-economic status).

In addition to the suggestions offered above, future research efforts should consider expanding this study to include licensed items of the Paralympic Games, but also products of other mega-events, such as the FIFA World Cup or the NFL Super Bowl. Research could also be conducted to directly explore differences in meanings between Olympic vs. non-Olympic licensed items as well as licensed items that are available year-round (e.g. by teams, collegiate athletic departments) vs. licensed items of unique events (e.g. Final Four championships, All-Star Games).

Note

1. Examples include "In the True Spirit of the Games", "Welcome Home".

References

Apostolopoulou, A. (2002). Brand extensions by U.S. professional sport teams: Motivations and keys to success. *Sport Marketing Quarterly*, *11*, 205–214.

Arnould, E.J., & Thompson, C.J. (2005). Consumer culture theory (CCT): Twenty years of research. *Journal of Consumer Research*, *31*(4), 868–882.

Athens 2004 Olympics: General Fact Sheet. (2004). *Athens 2004 Olympics: General Fact Sheet*. Retrieved March 12, 2009, from http://www.greekembassy.org/Embassy/content/en/Article.aspx?office=3&folder=95&article=12033.

Blumer, H. (1969). *Symbolic interactionism: Perspectives and method*. Englewood Cliffs, NJ: Prentice-Hall.

Bourdieu, P. (1984). *Distinction: A social critique of the judgment of taste*. Cambridge, MA: Harvard University Press.

Crawford, G. (2004). Consumer sport: Fans, sport and culture. *International Journal of Sport Marketing & Sponsorship*, *6*, 124–139.

Dacin, P.A., & Smith, D.C. (1994). The effect of brand portfolio characteristics on consumer evaluations of brand extensions. *Journal of Marketing Research*, *31*, 229–242.

de Cillia, R., Reisigl, M., & Wodak, R. (1999). The discursive construction of national identities. *Discourse & Society*, *10*, 149–173.

Douglas, M., & Isherwood, B. (1996). *The world of goods: Towards an anthropology of consumption*. London: Routledge.

Elliott, R. (1997). Existential consumption and irrational desire. *European Journal of Marketing*, *31*, 285–296.

Elliott, R., & Wattanasuwan, K. (1998). Brands as symbolic resource for the construction of identity. *International Journal of Advertising*, *17*, 131–145.

Fink, J.S., Trail, G.T., & Anderson, D.F. (2002). Environmental factors associated with spectator attendance and sport consumption behavior: Gender and team differences. *Sport Marketing Quarterly*, *11*(1), 8–19.

Fournier, S. (1998). Consumers and their brands: Developing relationship theory in consumer research. *Journal of Consumer Research*, *24*, 343–373.

Funk, D.C., & Pastore, D.L. (2000). Equating attitudes to allegiance: The usefulness of selected attitudinal information in segmenting loyalty to professional sports teams. *Sport Marketing Quarterly*, *9*(4), 175–184.

Gladden, J.M., & Funk, D.C. (2001). Understanding brand loyalty in professional sport: Examining the link between brand associations and brand loyalty. *International Journal of Sports Marketing & Sponsorship*, *3*, 67–94.

Gladden, J.M., Milne, G.R., & Sutton, W.A. (1998). A conceptual framework for assessing brand equity in Division I college athletics. *Journal of Sport Management*, *12*, 1–19.

Hogan, J. (2003). Staging the nation: Gendered and ethnicized discourses of national identity in Olympic opening ceremonies. *Journal of Sport and Social Issues*, *27*, 100–123.

Holbrook, M.B., & Hirschman, E.C. (1982). The experiential aspects of consumption: Consumer fantasies, feelings, and fun. *Journal of Consumer Research*, *9*, 132–140.

Holt, D.B. (1995). How consumers consume: A typology of consumption practices. *Journal of Consumer Research*, *22*, 1–16.

Horak, R., & Spitaler, G. (2003). Sport space and national identity: Soccer and skiing as formative forces: On the Austrian example. *American Behavioral Scientist, 46*, 1506–1518.

Kersting, N. (2007). Sport and national identity: A comparison of the 2006 and 2010 FIFA World Cups. *Politikon, 34*, 277–293.

Kwon, H.H., & Armstrong, K.L. (2006). Impulse purchase of sport team licensed merchandise: What matters? *Journal of Sport Management, 20*, 101–119.

Kwon, H.H., Kim, H., & Mondello, M. (2008). Does a manufacturer matter in co-branding? The influence of a manufacturer brand on sport team licensed apparel. *Sport Marketing Quarterly, 17*, 163–172.

Kwon, H., Trail, G.T., & Anderson, D.F. (2006). Points of attachment (identification) and licensed merchandise consumption among American college students. *International Journal of Sport Management, 7*, 347–360.

Kwon, H.H., Trail, G., & James, J.D. (2007). The mediating role of perceived value: Team identification and purchase intention of team-licensed apparel. *Journal of Sport Management, 21*, 540–554.

Ligas, M. (2000). People, products, and pursuits: Exploring the relationship between consumer goals and product meanings. *Psychology & Marketing, 17*, 983–1003.

Ligas, M., & Cotte, J. (1999). The process of negotiating brand meaning: A symbolic interactionist perspective. *Advances in Consumer Research, 26*, 609–614.

Maguire, J., Barnard, S., Butler, K., & Golding, P. (2008). 'Celebrate Humanity' or 'consumers?': A critical evaluation of a brand in motion. *Social Identities, 14*, 63–76.

Maguire, J., & Poulton, E.K. (1999). European identity politics in Euro 96: Invented traditions and national habitus codes. *International Review for the Sociology of Sport, 34*, 17–29.

McCracken, G. (1986). Culture and consumption: A theoretical account of the structure and movement of the cultural meaning of consumer goods. *Journal of Consumer Research, 13*, 71–84.

Mullin, B.J., Hardy, S., & Sutton, W.A. (2000). *Sport marketing* (2nd ed.). Champaign, IL: Human Kinetics.

Olympic Marketing Fact File. (2010). *Olympic licensing*. Retrieved January 24, 2010, from http://www.olympic.org/Documents/fact_file_2010.pdf.

Piacentini, M., & Mailer, G. (2004). Symbolic consumption in teenagers' clothing choices. *Journal of Consumer Behavior, 3*, 251–262.

Richins, M.L. (1994). Valuing things: The public and private meanings of possessions. *Journal of Consumer Research, 21*, 504–521.

Ross, S. (2006). A conceptual framework for understanding spectator-based brand equity. *Journal of Sport Management, 20*, 22–38.

Sewpaul, V. (2009). On national identity, nationalism and Soccer 2010: Should social work be concerned? *International Social Work, 52*, 143–153.

Solomon, M.R. (1983). The role of products as social stimuli: A symbolic interactionism perspective. *Journal of Consumer Behavior, 10*, 319–329.

Sports Business Resource Guide & Fact Book. (2009). *Licensing*. Street & Smith's Sports Group.

The Olympic Symbols. (2007). *The Olympic museum* (2nd ed.). Retrieved January 30, 2010, from http://multimedia.olympic.org/pdf/en_report_1303.pdf.

Thompson, C.J., & Haytko, D.L. (1997). Speaking of fashion: Consumers' uses of fashion discourses and the appropriation of countervailing cultural meanings. *Journal of Consumer Research, 24*, 15–22.

Tsoukalas, C. (1999). European modernity and Greek national identity. *Journal of Southern Europe and the Balkans, 1*, 7–14.

Tuck, J. (2003). The men in white: Reflections on rugby union, the media and Englishness. *International Review for the Sociology of Sport, 38*, 177–199.

Wann, D.L. (2002). Preliminary validation of a measure for assessing identification as a sport fan: The Sport Fandom Questionnaire. *International Journal of Sport Management, 3*, 103–115.

Wann, D.L., & Branscombe, N.R. (1993). Sports fans: Measuring degree of identification with their team. *International Journal of Sport Psychology, 24*, 1–17.

Embracing Cultural Contexts and Critical Reflexivity: (Re)presenting the Global Sports Industry in Research and Practice

STEVEN W. POPE

International Center for Performance Excellence, College of Physical Activity and Sport Sciences, West Virginia University, Morgantown, WV 26506, USA

ABSTRACT Management arises out of ordinary human relationships within which people make individual and collective choices based on their cultural values and beliefs. To date, however, there has been limited analysis of the centrality of "culture" and "cultural issues" within the social practice and scholarly study of sport management. The author champions the case for a more conceptually-reflexive approach to sport management in theory and practice—one rooted in the problematical engagement with "culture." It is argued that a "culturalist" approach would enable sport management students and practitioners to better understand the dynamics of diversity within the sports industry and the appropriate cross-cultural and multicultural skills needed. The development of cultural sensitivity within the field of sport management requires deliberate personal, theoretical, methodological and practice interventions. The article features the author's own personal journey toward embracing and articulating a wider historical, multicultural, critically-reflexive approach to the field of sport management. The author encourages practitioners to exude less certainty about the existing range of topics and program benchmarks and experiment more with conceptual approaches which engage the concepts of cultural identities and praxis.

Introduction

The influential historian and theorist Raymond Williams, who was a leading scholar of the history of English literary expression, famously maintained that the term "culture" is one of the most complex and confusing words in the English language. Throughout his multifaceted and often polemical scholarship Williams shifted the dominant view of "culture" as a privileged space of artistic production and specialist knowledge (e.g. "high culture") toward a broader understanding that "culture is a whole way of life". In his words, "culture is ordinary"—it is "the lived experience of the everyday" (quoted in Gray and McGuigan, 1997, pp. 5–6). The immediate scholarly and political context within which Williams proffered this approach was a raging debate within western Marxism about the relationship between the forces of production and the core assumptions and values held by individuals in particular societies. Between the 1960s and early 1980s, Williams and various other neo-Marxist scholars in the humanities and social sciences argued against a strictly economistic (and deterministic—"orthodox" Marxist) approach to culture and society.[1]

As a history graduate student during the late 1980s and early 1990s, I was profoundly influenced by the work of Williams, E. P. Thompson and Eric Hobsbawm, in particular (as well as various other, earlier European historians such as Marc Bloch and Fernand Braudel—associated with the French *Annales* tradition—and the Italian political theorist Antonio Gramsci). By the early to mid-1980s, a group of scholars steeped in western Marxism (primarily in Britain and the USA) developed a "cultural studies" approach to not only understanding the prevailing power relationships within societies (past and present) but linking their intellectual work with practice ("praxis"). The pioneering work of Stuart Hall et al. promoted interdisciplinary scholarship of social identities (as inflected through race, class, gender, sexuality) and the contested nature of power, difference and social justice—rooted in specific geographical and historical conjectures. A cultural studies approach is praxis-driven (not a purely academic endeavor but rather one that attempts to address real, contemporary socio-cultural-political issues) and self-reflexive (an approach that realizes the potential incongruity and transient nature of the knowledge it produces). My approach to the study of sport hails from this intellectual and epistemological tradition(s).

To date, the majority of sport management researchers and practitioners have not emerged from this intellectual background. As a result, there has been rather limited analysis of the centrality of "culture" and "cultural issues" within the social practice of sport management. Girginov writes that "culture and sport management are not separate entities", rather various interpretations of and methodological approaches within sport management are "cultural constructs underpinned by core assumptions and values held by members of professional communities in different countries". Management arises out of ordinary human relationships within which people make individual and collective choices based on their (cultural) values and beliefs. Thus, as Girginov argues, we cannot "fully comprehend why managers act the way they do without considering the *meaning* [my emphasis] they ascribe to their actions and the environments" (Girginov, 2009). A culturalist approach would, thus, generate local knowledge of problems to enable practitioners (and researchers) to better understand the dynamics of cultural diversity within the sports industry and the appropriate cross-cultural (multicultural) skills needed. The development of cultural sensitivity within the field of sport management requires deliberate personal, theoretical, methodological and practice interventions. What follows is merely traces of one person's journey into developing a wider, historical, multicultural, more critically-reflexive approach to "sport management".

Personal Point of Entry

My personal intervention with the "sport management cultures" thrust of this special issue began about four years ago upon being commissioned to edit a global handbook on sports history. I (along with co-editor John Nauright) began envisioning what such a text might look like in light of the ways in which our primary field (sports history) had developed over the past three decades. In developing the *Routledge Companion to Sports History*, we attempted to identify the major thematic and methodological trends that currently define the field and believed that, as organized sport has become globalized, it was essential to produce a more multicultural overview of sports history, which has too often been artificially constrained by national borders (and the attendant national-academic discourses). We reckoned that sports historians of the twenty-first century needed to understand the concerns of their colleagues in other parts of the world in order to advance the field into new areas of enquiry, analysis and conceptualization. The resulting *Companion* (published in late 2009 but bearing a 2010 copyright) provides abundant evidence of a "coming of age" story whereby a fledgling topical area that had been embraced by only a small handful of scholars prior to the early 1970s, became linked to the burgeoning "new" social history, flourished during the 1980s–1990s and ultimately achieved (at least partially) the long-sought "holy grail" of mainstream academic legitimacy. As scholars influenced by the broader "cultural turn" within the humanities and social sciences, we approached the selection of key topics and regional developments as part and parcel of the inherently selective and subjective nature of historical enquiry. Nevertheless, our goal was to create a reasonably "comprehensive", multicultural, and internationally-representative collection of freshly-conceived essays by established scholars around the world which would represent the diversity within academic sport history. In so doing, we attempted to provide an overview of how sport history as an academic enterprise has developed globally.[2] The end result of the *Companion*, though, was a broad representation of the major themes that have focused the minds of sports historians around the globe, as well as the areas where scholarship has developed rapidly in recent years.[3]

This experience was formative to our reflection upon the cultural, conceptual and methodological challenges in developing another volume—*The New Sport Management Reader*—for a global, multicultural audience in a different (albeit, related) disciplinary field. We initially came upon the idea for the project simultaneously through separate (albeit related) personal journeys. In both of our cases, we formulated views on the "future of sport management" for job interview presentations in 2007–2008.[4] Unbeknownst to each other at the time, we both canvassed the academic sport management literature and gauged the dominant and emergent discourses. We were both ultimately struck by two basic trends: what might be termed the dominant discourse which centered upon program/curricular certification and traditional (old-style with regard to the leading edge in the social sciences) positivist and functional analyses of the business of sport; but also a fledgling (albeit modest) discourse about the need for more searching, critically adventurous theoretical and methodological approaches within the field. Needless to say (based upon our training as historians and intellectual predilection toward cultural studies), we were both attracted to the emergent discourse—one which tended to arise not from the "usual suspects" but rather from critics within the discipline as well as interdisciplinary interlopers—all of whom noted the conceptually impoverished state of affairs within the otherwise thriving field of "sport management".

This emergent critique within and outside of sport management first commandeered my inspiration as the auspices for a book. As a new publishing director, I initially crafted a short list of editors to approach for designing a book that would hopefully nudge the field of sport management out of its conceptual slumber and into a new direction. After all, by virtue of being a "sport historian", I was not a proper card-carrying member of the "sport management" club. Once again, I consulted my erstwhile sports studies colleague John Nauright, who had experienced a similar epiphany regarding the future of sport management during precisely the same historical moment.[5]

The challenge of developing an anthology that might provoke sport management scholars to conceive of their enterprise in new ways proved to be a stimulating experience for us. We saw how the evolution of sport history and sport management as emerging areas exuded similarities and disparities. Both ultimately derived from physical education and became recognized subjects within the now more recognized discipline of kinesiology (although both areas derive their scholarly vitality from practitioners in history and business/management); and how both were initially derided as ephemeral areas of study within the established, "mainstream" disciplines of history and management. Yet, whereas the once buoyant "humanities" component within physical education and kinesiology departments shrivelled due to the ascendancy of "exercise science" and "administration", "sport management" (unlike "sport history") prospered, due in large measure to its perceived career quotient (Booth, 1997). Sport management is a relatively young field as academic areas of study go.[6] Research on the business aspects of sport is not limited to these associations and their journals, however. A vibrant scholarship has emerged that examines the many facets of the sports industry internationally within sport history and sport sociology in particular and that informs and contextualizes research within "sport management". Yet, with the increase in student enrolment in sport management since the 1990s, the core focus of the field has evolved to the point whereby professional training components have been elevated while simultaneously, critical, interdisciplinary training has been marginalized. As John Amis and Michael Silk (2005) contend

> what currently holds the center in sport management research is a somewhat narrow definition of the field that, in many ways, blinkers sport management scholars in their ability and potential to provide a critical examination of the operations and machinations of sport-related industries and institutions"[7]

We found this development problematical for the long-term health of sport management as a viable scholarly realm and, as such, were inspired to develop *The New Sport Management Reader* as a clarion call for a more critical, reflexive approach to sport management education and practice for the future.

Unlike our work in developing the *Companion*, we approached a disciplinary field of sport management as one that had not developed internationally to the extent that had sport history. The epicenter of the sport management scholarship was still a very much transatlantic (US–UK) one, with the overwhelming majority of the literature published in the US. Although there are some fledgling, regional critical masses developing in Europe and Australasia, there simply was not the heft of published scholarship to gauge a truly global overview of the field. Moreover, similar to our experience in developing the *Companion*, we (as two almost exclusively English-speaking scholars) privileged work in our native language (at the expense of excavating, in the case of the *Reader*, cross-cultural analyses published in other languages). Americans' lack of facility in non-English languages remains an obstacle to comparative intellectual work in all humanities and social sciences disciplines. In the end, we attempted to provide a *representative* selection of scholarship from the recognized core areas of focus within sport management research globally. Methodologically speaking, unlike our work on the *Companion* (where we contacted an international group of contributors for commissioned, new essays), we selected from previously-published works for the *Reader*. We were especially interested in selecting pieces that engaged with the *broader social consequences* of sport, be they economic or environmental or issues related to human rights—which we believe are fundamental and ought to be at the forefront of planning and programming in sport management.

The resulting *Reader* is what might be characterized as a "socio-cultural" approach to sport management that calls into question the dominant orthodoxy in sport management—particularly as it has been practiced in North America and which has taken hold in other regions of the world, notably parts of Europe and in Australia and New Zealand. It urges sport management professionals to critically examine the range of sport programs and policies with which they are actively engaged on a daily basis and to constantly ask "why" and "for whom" is sport being played? As Robert Rinehart (1998) reminds us, we are "players all" in this game we call sports and there are certainly social, political, economic, cultural, environmental and many other consequences of how we "do" sport individually and collectively.

Selected Cultural/Multicultural "Findings" from the *Reader*

In what briefly follows, I wish to merely highlight some of the key methodological implications emerging from the *Reader* so as to engage with the complex links between culture (in its various manifestations) and global sport management—which is the central thrust of this particular special issue of *ESMQ* (as well as the underlying preoccupation with this particular contribution).

The most resounding "finding" (and perhaps polemically speaking "call to action") emerging from the *New Sport Management Reader* concerns method. The mainstream of sport management methodology continues to be dominated by positivist theoretical positions and functionalist conceptions of society. Former editor of the *Journal of Sport Management*, Frisby (2005) has argued that sport management research must be conducted from multiple paradigms. Without a critical perspective and method for evaluating marketing, accounting, human resource management and the like, practitioners and students alike miss the sheer messiness, the ambiguity and the politicized and fragmented nature of sport management. When students are trained primarily in the technical functions of organizational planning, organizing and controlling events and processes—without appropriate attention to the prevailing cultural, historical, economic and political contexts characterized by asymmetrical power relations—they are ill-equipped to think outside the textbook box. Frisby recommends a wider use of critical social science inquiry that "goes beyond surface illusions to uncover the real structures of the material world in order to help people change conditions and build a better world for themselves" (Frisby, 2005, p. 9).

This perspective is either implicitly or explicitly reinforced by most of the contributors to the *Reader*—most of whom embrace a commitment to critical, interdisciplinary theory and methodology for better conceptualizing sport management practices. Such contributions to the emergent critique of the field are intent on interrogating the dominant explanatory frameworks currently deployed within sport management and, as such, envision "a messier, challenging environment in which competing ontological, epistemological, and political positions exist alongside one another", which promises to "expand our intellectual horizons and offer the additional theoretical and practical insights that our rapidly developing field requires" (Amis and Silk, 2005, pp. 355–356).

The collection provides some illuminative examples of qualitative approaches underpinned by critical social theory. Singer (2009) explicates how critical race theory provides a useful tool for articulating the significance of race and ethnicity as viable epistemological considerations and challenges sport management scholars to better expand their horizons and thereby problematize the relationship between race and sport management and, in so doing, conceive of practical actions which could improve sport management research, theory and practice. Aitchison (2009) directs attention away from the prevailing organizational structures privileged within sport management research and calls for feminist and gender research which acknowledges and investigates the complexities of gendered power inherent in these mutually informing social and cultural relationships.

Other analyses direct attention to various qualitative approaches that have received short shrift within sport management research, such as ethnography, "thick description" (e.g. a Geertzian anthropological approach), historical research, political economy, legal research, as well as active engagement with deconstructionism. Giulianotti (2009) provides a typology of football fans and consumers by basing his theoretically derived from the work of earlier neo-Marxist approaches (conspicuously neglected within mainstream sport management) on the commodification process and thereby, providing an imminently useful model for differentiating supporters, fans, followers and *flâneurs* for further research in other sports. Schultz's (2009) historical analysis of the importance of the Mexican–Texan borderland region for understanding the ways in which local, regional and national identities are formed, challenged and constituted provides an invaluable reminder of essentializing national sporting cultures. He shows how a particular sport can be dominant within a national region and the ways in which, like the country itself, all identities—personal, local, regional, border, consumer, gender, racial—are contested, contradictory and in constant change. And, Nauright and Phillips (2009) remind us of how historically Australian football had not been privatized and that ownership had deliberately remained with the state-based institutions, clubs and members in part to resist takeover by global media interests (such as Murdoch's "Super League" scheme that fundamentally transferred one of Australia's key spectator sports from public ownership to the private model). Their piece was originally written at the time when the lure of North American sporting models and the attraction of North American sporting team apparel began to affect the Australian market but, simultaneously, they noted the widespread resistance to the wholesale adoption of North American ownership and marketing structures.

Several contributors highlight the *realpolitic* workings in play within the global sport industry and direct attention to the importance of the geography of social (and corresponding power) relations and how urban sporting and non-sporting spaces are being structured by particular political-economic and socio-cultural practices associated with the hosting of sporting mega-events. In their study of how cities are aggressively competing against each other to attract capital (and the way in which sport has become a key resource in this process), Duquette and Mason (2009) call for a more acute understanding of how elites in the urban regime see themselves as a strategic group and how members of local sporting communities network and interact with a city's broader business and political community. In their case study of the 2000 Sydney Olympics and the 1999 FIFA Under-17 World Soccer Championship, Scherer, Sam, and Batty (2009) document the increasingly prominent strategies employed by sporting organizations, local organizing committees and local governments to control sporting spaces and protect the interests of multinational sponsors from ambush marketing and thereby create hermetically-sealed branded/consumption sporting environments (in the interests of global capital which are often antithetical to free market principles).

Finally, in this whirlwind sampling of approaches and themes contained within the *Reader*, is a crucially important but heretofore neglected aspect within sport management research and practice—human rights. For far too long, the curriculum and research agenda has been stilted overwhelmingly toward "management" (and at the expense of "labor" which includes athletes). Dabscheck (2009) provides a historical overview of the human rights dimensions of sporting industrial relations since the late nineteenth century (at a time when many of the prevailing legal/management precedents were established in North America, Britain, Western Europe and Australia). From their inception, professional sports administrators and officials adopted rules which severely limited the human rights and economic freedom of athletes/players who have historically resented such controls and power relationships (and have consistently sought to mitigate and bring about the often draconian practices' abolition). Professional athletes (primarily team players in the dominant sports) have successfully challenged management through the court system through collective action (and have achieved, for example, collective bargaining rights). However, according to Dabscheck (2009), this window, which has enabled players of professional team sports to make use of collective action, would close if the sports leagues adopted employment rules consistent with various human rights instruments developed by the international community.

Beyond the realm of professionalized sport, the struggle for human rights within amateur sports has also been waged through the legal system as well as through grassroots activism targeted to broader changes in sport governance policy. Women's sport governance is an under-researched area within sport management research (and curriculum) internationally. Even within the minimalist, existing research there has been a failure to conceptually connect the advancement of women's sport to the prevailing (nationally-based) governance schemes. The dominant narrative regarding women's sport within the international sport management literature has been focused upon the steady increase in female participation (as if such numbers are signs of steady "progress"). Yet, according to Adams and Stevens (2009, p. 332),

> by shifting the focus from participation to governance, it is possible to identify how shortcomings still exist for women and girls in hockey Canada. Effective change is not simply a matter of increasing female hockey registration numbers; rather, it relates directly to issues of power and authority over sport which is intricately connected to governance structures.

As a strategy to address such a concern, they advocate "a fresh and creative approach that integrates a critical feminist perspective with a grassroots democratic focus (Adams and Stevens, 2009, p. 319). Whereas unlike the generally up-beat tone of the struggle for gender equity discourse within the US, policies for women's sport in the UK and throughout Europe have not been as effective as they could have been, according to

Breckenridge (2009), because of apathy towards gender equity. She notes, however, that child sexual abuse (in sport) *has* grabbed the media headlines in the UK and, as she argues, has the potential to open up debate on related rights issues across the equality "strands" and as such, that "child protection may turn out to be the lever for change that has eluded those groups seeking to promote women's rights in sport. At the same time it might deflect both attention and resources away from women's sports" (Breckenridge, 2009, p. 570). MacNeill, Donnelly, and Knight (2009) utilize ethnography to analyze the power relations between Canadian national team athletes, media, sponsors and sporting officials in preparation for the Sydney Games and the attendant relationships between the Canadian media, swimmers and sponsors. The institutionalization of a public relations training protocol functioned as a gate-keeping system to control media access to athletes (denying athletes constitutional rights to freedom of expression). The authors argue that public relations training needs to be resisted first and foremost within a human rights perspective so as to achieve an athlete-centered approach to high performance sport and to democratize the relationships between athletes, national sporting organizations, media and sponsors that are currently imbalanced in the exclusive rights setting (MacNeill et al, 2009).

Finally, researchers who place sport management within the material contexts of everyday life and multi-racial, economic and political democracy can, as Henry, Amara, Al-Tauqi, and Lee (2005) maintain, effectively address the imperatives of consumption; the dynamics of the marketplace; commercial space; the sweeping reach of neo-liberal ideology, power and influence; the production of knowledges and identities; nation-states; globalization; freedom; and community (Henry et al., 2005). They articulate the importance of international sports policy development and governance and the corresponding need for sustained comparative analysis. Such comparative, cross-cultural analyses must move beyond casual references to "globalization" toward a more critical analysis of the process. Neubauer (2009) delineates six fundamental, interconnected dynamics of globalization: collapse of time and space; migration and urbanization; wealth creation and distribution; transformation of global media; trade and consumption; and the transformation of value, and demonstrates how one might incorporate these characteristics within an analysis of a particular sport/management event (in this case, the 2008 Beijing Olympic Games).

Again, these selective themes highlighted from the *Reader* pertaining to race, gender, power relations, equity, human rights, geography and the like are visible and indicative characteristics of "culture", which enable sport management scholars to better frame (and problematize) their research in a more critical, conceptual framework. "Race", "class", "gender", "human rights", for example, are not merely static (functional or positivistic) categories, but rather, relational processes which enable us to better understand and explain prevailing values, beliefs and assumptions surrounding the management of sport. From a culturally-contextual conceptual perspective, these concepts are not ephemeral "window dressing" to be merely draped upon the "core" issues within sport management scholarship/curriculum/practice. Rather, they represent both real and heuristic issues which should inform practice. If taken seriously, such cultural characteristics should inform our methodology (as they concern matters of ontology and epistemology), practice—as well as (re)shape our world view(s).[8]

One Way Forward and an Illustrative Model

Unlike some sister disciplinary fields (such as sport history, sport sociology, and sport psychology), there has been very limited debate within sport management on the implications of the "cultural turn" on theory, methodology and epistemology.[9] How might mainstream sport management move this interpretive project forward? Zeigler (2007), one of the early pioneers of the field, advocates the need for a more critical definition of "sport" which would enable sport management scholars to make the important, interdisciplinary connections within sport studies as well as the wider social scientific disciplines. Sport management research tends to be constructed from an essentialized concept of "sport"—a fixed and immutable category—one that is primarily neutral and value-free with passing attention to the prevailing historical, political and cultural contexts. The dominant approach within the sport management discipline continues to posit the ways in which "sport" reflects "society" (society represents a huge entity with sport sitting upon it as a protuberance) rather than seeing the constitutive structures of sport as a social practice which are indissolubly connected to those that govern the whole of cultural and political life.[10] In contrast, according to Cashmore (2000, p. vii), sports are fluid and ever-changing "products of cultural endeavors, enterprises that have been manufactured in particular kinds of historical and social circumstances". To bring a more critical approach to sport, then, requires an awareness of a sporting practice's "interrelation with the social formations in which it is located and contested," as Andrews and Giardina (2008, p. 395) maintain—thus, "rather than seeking to develop some universal definition of sport, a more productive interpretive strategy is to locate particular sport forms and physical cultural experiences in the socio-historical context within which they came to exist".

As scholars who employ a cultural studies approach to the study of sport, Andrews and Giardina (2008) point to the way in which scholars are *cultural agents* in the very act of adopting certain definitions, methodologies and approaches toward their subject matter. As such, the act of identifying and embracing contextual cultural values as suggested in this article have potentially revolutionary implications for (re)shaping our interpretations and practices within sport management. According to Andrews and Giardina (2008, p. 406), the very act of articulation "involves a method reconstructing a cultural practice's conjunctural relations, identity, and effects to produce a contextually specific map of the social formation". With regard to a more critical articulation of "sport" and the field of "sport management", to operate within a contextual cultural studies strategy means "recognizing that sport forms (practices, products, institutions, etc.) can only be understood by the way that they are articulated into a particular set of complex social, economic, political, and technological relationships that compose the social context" (Andrews & Giardina, 2008, p. 406).

I wish to conclude this piece with an illuminative example of a framework that has been constructed at the intersections of sport history, sport management and cultural studies. As arguably the leading "culturalist" sport management scholar to date, Hardy has demonstrated how one can embrace a historical and global vision of sport and explain its management in an interdisciplinarily-nuanced fashion (informed by an engagement with the cultural theoretical approaches of Raymond Williams and Fernand Braudel to whom I referred at the outset but also constructed upon his experience as a sports administrator).

Hardy (1986, pp. 27–28) defines sport as a "triple" or "three-part" commodity. "These parts", he explains, "which can exist in isolation but which reach full expression in combination are . . . the activity or game form, the service and the goods".[11] In contextualizing this definition within the long history of sport (and the would-be global "sports industry"), Hardy, Loy, and Booth (2009, p. 132) have discerned six essential residuals:

- *agon* (the core contest between opposing individuals and/or teams);
- craft (the skills, practices and technologies required to achieve the *agon*istic dimension of competitive sport);
- community (the ways in which both athletes and spectators create bonds and bridges that simultaneously link and separate groups through shared sporting passions);
- gambling (the wagering on the outcome of the *agon*, which drives much of the passion surrounding sport);
- *eros* (the sexual attraction of "agonal" bodies); and
- framing (the tendency to surround the *agon* with frames of spectacle and festival, each of which contains elements of the other residual practices.[12]

Hardy maintains that these six systems of practice and belief have extended throughout historical time and geographical space by means of endless repetitions of performance. These six key residuals provide a useful model for contextualizing the history of sport management—one which integrates an appreciation of multiculturalism, tradition, power relationships, struggles over innovation, etc. Much of this history (of what might now be termed "sport management") is contained in the essentially *material culture* [my emphasis] of sport. Again, Hardy et al. (2009) provide a new typology:

- Playing equipment
- Venues
- Training equipment and sport medicine technology
- Sportswear
- Prizes
- Symbolic artefacts
- Performance measurement technology

- Ephemera
- Memorabilia

Space does not permit an elaboration upon these typological elements within the history and management of sport. Nevertheless, all of these components have been central to the management of sport in varying degrees since antiquity and, as such, should be part of the lexicon and knowledge of all sport managers in the twenty-first century (Hardy et al., 2009, p. 132). As Hardy et al. (2009) note "the material culture of any era is clearly influenced by conditions specific to time and place", nevertheless they contend that

> prizes, equipment, apparel, ephemera, arenas, and stadiums also reveal longer-term forms of thinking and acting. *Agon*, craft, community festival, spectacle, gambling, and *eros* have been stitched into colors, injected into balls, and embedded in the venues of sport across centuries and continents (Hardy et al., 2009, p. 148).[13]

Conclusion

At the end of this (perhaps overly) personalized, pedantic, politicized, proscribed, polemical (but hopefully not pedestrian) essay, I hope to have made the case for a more conceptually-imaginative approach to sport management in theory and practice—one rooted in the problematical engagement with "culture". As an offspring (perhaps an orphan) of physical education, sport studies and business studies, the field of sport management has matured into advanced adolescence as an academic area of study and occupation. While there is much to celebrate in this disciplinary and occupational evolution, there is also abundant reason to (re)consider both the *modus operandi* and *raison d'être* within the field.

For the primarily European readers of this journal, I recommend less deference to the well-established mainstream American disciplinary proclivities and more active engagement with continental approaches rooted in cultural-theoretical and cross-cultural analyses. What is needed for the future of sport management scholarship is greater theoretical and conceptual reflexivity—less certainty about the established topics and benchmarks and more experimentation and conceptual innovation which engages with cultural identities and praxis.

Zeigler (2007, p. 297) provocatively suggests:

> What are we [in sport management] helping to promote and exactly why are we doing it? I fear that we are simply going along with the seemingly inevitable tide. In the process, we have become pawns to the prevailing sport establishment by riding the wrong horse.

As sport management scholars, what is our role within the context of the global sports industry? Have we become merely "pawns" and apologists or can we (re)claim a role as agents of cultural change? If the latter, let us embrace the reins informed by the importance of culture and steer the field of sport management in a more critical direction.

Acknowledgements

Some of the material in this article has appeared in Pope and Nauright (2010, pp. 3–11) and Nauright and Pope (2009, pp. xvii–xxiv). I wish to acknowledge John Nauright's incisive work on these two books which help to inform the first section of this article. I also wish to gratefully acknowledge Vassil Girginov's incisive comments and support for this essay.

Notes

1. For a couple of useful overviews of this critical debate, see Anderson (1980) and Kaye (1984).
2. Although we were well aware that the national/regional organizing schematic may (unduly) compartmentalize analysis, we realized that much of the sport historiography remains nationally focused. As Editors, we are both English speakers and, therefore, the collection is biased towards sports history written in the English language and coverage of sporting cultures in countries where English is the first language. As a result, the *Companion* was not fully comprehensive (an allusive goal which could not be achieved in a single volume covering sports history around the world). Some of this can be attributed to contributors pulling out along the way, not being able to submit their commissioned pieces on time or simply not being able to adequately cover the desired topic at all. The other constraint lies in finding scholars with the time frame to write a detailed piece in a second or third language.
3. For a more detailed discussion of these issues, see Pope and Nauright (2010, pp. 3–11), as well as prominent social historian Peter Stearns' (2010, pp. x–xv) insightful "Foreword".
4. I interviewed for the position of Director of the International Center for Performance Excellence within which the publishing operation of Fitness Information Technology (FiT) is situated. FiT is a leading publisher of books and journals in the area of sport management.
5. Nauright's Power Point presentation at GMU characterized the field of sport management in 2007 as essentially divided between two major schools of thought—applied research (particularly within marketing and sponsorship) and the operation of sport as a social institution and technology, as well as the ethical, moral and social implications of sport. John was primarily interested in the latter school of thought within the field and thereby focused his presentation on the following themes (which underpinned his widely-varied and ambitious personal research agenda): political economy of sport; globalization and sport management; international sport management; sport, events and tourism; and sports development. His "Vision for the Future of Sport Mangement" Power Point file is in this author's possession.
6. The North American Society for Sport Management (NASSM) was founded in 1985 and organized its first conference a year later. The European Association for Sport Management (EASM) was established in 1993, while the Sport Management Association of Australia and New Zealand (SMAANZ) emerged in 1995. Together these three associations form the International Sport Management Alliance. Some of the key sport studies journals include the *Journal of Sport History*, *International Journal of the History of Sport*, *Sport History Review*, *Sociology of Sport Journal*, *International Review of the Sociology of Sport*, *Journal of Sport and Social Issues*, *Sporting Traditions* and *Sport in Society*. In addition to the vast periodical literature in sport studies there is an expansive body of specialized monographs, edited collections and invaluable reference books dealing with the social and historical development of the global sports industry.

7. For an another preliminary effort of setting a more comparative, international research agenda, see the special issue on "Sport management and marketing at the global–local nexus", edited by S. Jackson (2005).
8. I wish to thank V. Girginov for helping me to articulate this point.
9. For an authoritative statement, see Zeigler (2007). For a detailed examination of the development of methodology within sport history, see Booth (2005) and Pope and Nauright (2010). For incisive evaluations of sport sociology past and present, see Gruneau (1999), Ingham and Donnelly (1997, pp. 364–395) and Andrews (2008). For a review of developments within sport psychology, see Ryba, Schinke and Tenenbaum (2009).
10. The classic and pioneering discussion of this comes from Richard Gruneau's (1983) *Sport, Class and Social Development* (see the 1999 edition with an Afterword in which Gruneau considers the book fifteen years later). For a valuable overview of the development of a contextual, relational (cultural studies) approach to "sport", see King (2005).
11. For an excellent, recent overview of the history of sports entrepreneurship, see Porter (2010).
12. Hardy originally introduced a model closely akin to this one twenty years earlier in his pioneering exploration "Entrepreneurs, Structures, and the Sportgeist" (1990).
13. For an earlier, but still useful, primer on a "culturalist" approach to sport, see Hardy and Ingham (1993).

References

Adams, C., & Stevens, J. (2009). Change and grassroots movement: Reconceptualizing women's hockey governance in Canada. In J. Nauright, & S.W. Pope (Eds.), *The new sport management reader* (pp. 317–336). Morgantown: Fitness Information Technology.

Aitchison, C. (2009). Feminist and gender research in sport and leisure management: Understanding the social–cultural nexus of gender-power relations. In J. Nauright, & S.W. Pope (Eds.), *The new sport management reader* (pp. 25–46). Morgantown: Fitness Information Technology.

Amis, J., & Silk, M. (2005). Rupture: Promoting critical and innovative approaches to the study of sport management. *Journal of Sport Management, 19*, 355–366.

Anderson, P. (1980). *Arguments within English Marxism.* London: Verso.

Andrews, D. (2008). Kinesiology's "inconvenient truth" and the physical cultural studies imperative. *Quest, 60*(1), 45–62.

Andrews, D., & Giardina, M. (2008). Sport without guarantees: Toward a cultural studies that matters. *Cultural Studies–Critical Methodologies, 8*(4), 395–422.

Booth, D. (1997). Sport history: What can be done? *Sport, Education and Society*, 2, 191–204.

Booth, D. (2005). *The field: Truth and fiction in sport history.* London: Routledge.

Breckenridge, C. (2009). Women and children first? Child abuse and child protection in sport. In J. Nauright, & S.W. Pope (Eds.), *The new sport management reader* (pp. 559–573). Morgantown: Fitness Information Technology.

Cashmore, E. (2000). *Sports culture: An A–Z guide.* London: Routledge.

Dabscheck, B. (2009). Sport, human rights, and industrial relations. In J. Nauright, & S.W. Pope (Eds.), *The new sport management reader* (pp. 337–362). Morgantown: Fitness Information Technology.

Duquette, G., & Mason, D. (2009). Urban regimes sport in North American cities: Seeking status through franchises, events, and facilities. In J. Nauright, & S.W. Pope (Eds.), *The new sport management reader* (pp. 65–85). Morgantown: Fitness Information Technology.

Frisby, W. (2005). The good, the bad, and the ugly: Critical sport management research. *Journal of Sport Management, 19*, 1–12.

Girginov, V. (2009). Call for papers "sport management cultures" for the *European Sport Management Quarterly*. Retrieved January 1, 2010, from http://www.tandf.co.uk/journals/cfp/resmcfp.pdf.

Giulianotti, R. (2009). Supporters, followers, fans, and flaneurs: A taxonomy of spectator identities in football. In J. Nauright, & S.W. Pope (Eds.), *The new sport management reader* (pp. 209–229). Morgantown: Fitness Information Technology.

Gray, A., & McGuigan, J. (Eds.) (1997). *Studying culture: An introductory reader*. London: Arnold.

Gruneau, R. (1999). A postscript 15 years later. In *Class, sports, and social development* (2nd ed.). Champaign: Human Kinetics.

Hardy, S. (1986). Entrepreneurs, organizations and the sport marketplace: Subjects in search of historians. *Journal of Sport History*, *13*, 14–33.

Hardy, S. (1990). Entrepreneurs, structures, and the sportgeist: Old tensions in a modern industry. In D. Kyle, & G. Stark (Eds.), *Essays on sport history and sport mythology* (pp. 45–82). College Station, Texas: A & M Press.

Hardy, S., & Ingham, A. (1993). Introduction: Sport studies through the lens of Raymond Williams. In A. Ingham, & J. Loy (Eds.), *Sport in social development: Traditions, transitions, and transformations* (pp. 1–19). Champaign: Human Kinetics.

Hardy, S., Loy, J., & Booth, D. (2009). The material culture of sport: Toward a typology. *Journal of Sport History*, *36*, 129–140.

Henry, I., Amara, M., Al-Tauqi, M., & Lee., P.C. (2005). A typology of approaches to comparative analysis of sports policy. *Journal of Sport Management*, *19*, 480–496.

Ingham, A., & Donnelly, P. (1997). A sociology of North American sociology of sport: Disunity in unity, 1965–1996. *Sociology of Sport Journal*, *14*, 362–418.

Jackson, S. (2005). Sport management and marketing at the global–local nexus. Special Issue. *International Journal of Sport Management and Marketing*, *1*(1/2), 3–189.

Kaye, H. (1984). *The British Marxist historians*. New York: Polity Press.

King, S. (2005). Methodological contingencies in sports studies. In D. Andrews, et al. (Eds.), *Qualitative methods in sports studies* (pp. 21–38). London: Berg.

MacNeill, M., Donnelly, P., & Knight, G. (2009). Corporate training: Identity construction, preparation for the Sydney Olympic Games and relationships between Canadian media, swimmers, and sponsors. In J. Nauright, & S.W. Pope (Eds.), *The new sport management reader* (pp. 401–427). Morgantown: Fitness Information Technology.

Nauright, J., & Phillips, M. (2009). Us and them: Australian professional sport and resistance to North American ownership and marketing models. In J. Nauright, & S.W. Pope (Eds.), *The new sport management reader* (pp. 265–275). Morgantown: Fitness Information Technology.

Nauright, J., & Pope, S.W. (Eds.) (2009). *The new sport management reader*. Morgantown: Fitness Information Technology.

Neubauer, D. (2009). Modern sport and Olympic Games: The problematic complexities raised by the dynamics of globalization. In J. Nauright, & S.W. Pope (Eds.), *The new sport management reader* (pp. 463–497). Morgantown: Fitness Information Technology.

Pope, S.W., & Nauright, J. (Eds.) (2010). *The Routledge companion to sports history*. London: Routledge.

Porter, D. (2010). Entrepeneurship. In Pope, S.W., & Nauright, J. (Eds.), *The Routledge companion to sports history* (pp. 197–215). London: Routledge.

Rinehart, R. (1998). *Players all: Performances in contemporary society*. Bloomington: Indiana University Press.

Ryba, T.V., Schinke, R., & Tenenbaum, G. (2009). *The cultural turn in sport psychology*. Morgantown: Fitness Information Technology.

Scherer, J., Sam, M., & Batty, R. (2009). Sporting sign wars: Advertising and the contested terrain of sporting events and venues. In J. Nauright, & S.W. Pope (Eds.), *The new sport management reader* (pp. 133–153). Morgantown: Fitness Information Technology.

Schultz, R. (2009). El rey de Los Deportes: Bodies, business and border identities in Mexican baseball. In J. Nauright, & S.W. Pope (Eds.), *The new sport management reader* (pp. 231–248). Morgantown: Fitness Information Technology.

Singer, J. (2009). Addressing epistemological racism in sport management research. In J. Nauright, & S.W. Pope (Eds.), *The new sport management reader* (pp. 47–64). Morgantown: Fitness Information Technology.

Stearns, P. (2010). Foreword. In S.W. Pope, & J. Nauright (Eds.), *The Routledge companion to sports history* (pp. x–xv). London: Routledge.

Zeigler, E. (2007). Sport management must show social concern as it develops tenable theory. *Journal of Sport Management*, *21*, 297–318.

Epilogue: Sport Management Research as a Culture of Knowledge and Ignorance Creation

VASSIL GIRGINOV

School of Sport & Education, Brunel University, Middlesex, UK

The *Sport Management Cultures* collection set to explore the explanatory power of the culture concept for the study and practice of sport management. This has never been systematically attempted in the field of sport management before. To that end, six original contributions have shed light on culture and its relationship with various aspects of management including its conceptualisation, policies, organisational behaviour and symbolic interpretations. Thus, it is expected that after reading the volume most readers will feel better informed and that hopefully some of their previously held assumptions about this topic will be challenged. Ultimately, it is for the reader to judge to what extent the objectives of this collection have been achieved.

This concluding part looks at the other side of the process of systematic knowledge creation and touches on the patterns of ignorance production that always exist alongside it. A true commitment to the culture concept compels us to do so, as research in sport management is culturally determined in terms of ontologies, themes and social organisation. Advances in knowledge in this field are culturally distinctive as are the patterns of ignorance. North American sport management research is far more advanced in areas such as marketing and business, which is in-line with the strong ethos of individualism, competitiveness and strive for commoditisation of life that defines American culture. Conversely, one finds that most systematic accounts on voluntary sport organisations and social capital have been produced by European commentators. This, too, is in keeping with a strong voluntary tradition underpinned by concerns for equality and autonomy that is characteristic of a culture of greater community spirit and state support for sport in many European societies. Sport management research therefore, could be viewed as a culture in its own right, which is equally responsible for advancing and hindering knowledge production. Every time a research agenda to investigate a specific sport management phenomenon is set it means that a choice has been made to do that from a particular point of view, and at the expense of other perspectives, themes and issues, which could have been researched. As Harding (1998, p. 56) expresses it "culture in some respects functions as a prison house for the growth of knowledge, in other respects culture is the tool box that enables valuable though always local knowledge about natural and social worlds". The research choices we make are determined by explicit and implicit epistemological and ontological perspectives that underpin different cultures and shape the local sport systems. Whatever the epistemological point of view, management is a normative system with its own parameters as to what counts as valuable knowledge, as argued in the introductory chapter. For example, the recent preoccupation with evidence-based approaches to policy, management and development of sport in the West, has been grounded in a cultural belief in scientific rationality and that such evidence enhances democratic governance by ensuring greater transparency and accountability of individual and organisational actions. However, privileging scientific overlay knowledge in sport management is a value laden proposition and a hugely problematic one. It is also a culturally-determined position suggesting that knowledge is in general preferable to ignorance. Often, however, by prioritising knowledge produced by professionals we ignore lay persons' subjective experiences, because these are harder to quantify and measure, and subsequently used to inform policies (Haas, 2004).

The importance of the 'human side of management', which considers people as creators of management knowledge, has been argued by generations of scholars from Barnard, to Simon, Mayo, Drucker, Weick, Peters & Waterman, Mintzberg and Alvesson. Nonaka & Takeuchi (1995) noted the limitations of the Western epistemological tradition in management as being concerned with "the acquisition, accumulation and utilization of *existing* knowledge; they lack the perspective of 'creating new knowledge'" (p.49) (emphasis in original). The point is that sport management does not need to be concerned only with explicit, that is, with formal and systemic knowledge. Equal attention ought to be afforded to the tacit knowledge in the form of subjective insights and intuitions, which entails drawing from local and culturally meaningful sources and experiences. The duality of explicit and tacit knowledge is akin to the tension between culture's simultaneous striving for singularization and homogenization. The promotion of sport participation nicely captures this tension. While sport managers try to develop homogeneous messages about the benefits of sport to be shared by everybody, at the same time they also aspire to translate those messages to individuals and groups, by singling them out and concentrating on their unique characteristics and life styles. This cultural tension has wider political and governance implications concerned with how to make sense out of a universe of diverse cultures while preserving social control in sport.

Thibault's (2010) review of the global field of sport management suggests that, its development has been progressive, and is currently boosting some 347 undergraduate and graduate programmes worldwide. In addition, there are 12 dedicated academic journals in the English language covering seven substantial aspects of the field including, management, marketing, events, finance and economics, communication, policy and pedagogy. However, this growth should not conceal the academic tribalism in sport management, which is also responsible for establishing patterns of ignorance. This issue is particularly well-manifested in the social organisation of sport management departments, curricula and research agendas. These typically revolve around a limited number of aspects of sport management centered on the research interests of core staff, and tend to ignore the development of new areas in the field and the appointment of academics that do not fit in those established categories. This is a cultural, as much as an ontological and epistemological issue, in that both people and organisations struggle to accommodate alternative views of sport management.

Every Sport Manager has its own Management Gospel

Writing some 30 years ago Laurent (1983) observed: "I realised that any attempt to communicate alternative ideas about the process of management was headed for failure if it could not in some way first address the implicit management gospel that managers carried in their heads" (p.75). The implicit management gospel concerns, of course, managers' own ontological and epistemological assumptions and ideologies that help them make sense of the world around them. It can be discerned at organisational, sub-cultural and culture-generic level, and supports the point that management ideologies and beliefs guide action. Laurent's comment further reinforces the view that management gospels, apart from assisting people to navigate in the complex world of sport, also produce patterns of ignorance by asserting particular taken-for-granted models of work that are representative of dominant gender, class or race ideologies (Nkomo, 1992). Getting managers to alter their visions and modes of operation is a cultural challenge as it involves change in subjectivity. Here we enter the innovative aspect of culture where the core task is change management. Change management concerns not only developing new sport cultures, organisational structures, programmes and identities, but changing managers' own ideologies as well. Frequently, resistance to change comes more from within the members of an organisation than from the people whose behaviour we try to address through sport. A number of studies on organisational change in a range of cultural contexts including Australia, Bulgaria, Canada and the UK (Amis & Slack, 2002, Caza, 2000, Girginov & Sandanski, 2008, Kikulis, 2000, Skinner, Stewart, & Edwards, 1999), clearly showed that managers and organisations actively resist cultural change. What is more, O'Reilly & Knight (2007) point out that sport managers not only prefer to stick to their management gospels but are generally unwilling to share their knowledge with others.

MacIntosh, Doherty and Walker, in this volume, demonstrated the existence of industry-wide culture in the Canadian fitness sector. This culture is based on shared assumptions, beliefs and values, which together form the gospel of the managers working in this industry. But as the authors indicate, this gospel may not be shared by all members of the fitness industry due to sub-cultural differences, and as a result they will find it difficult to navigate in an environment which promotes different working standards. Amara and Henry, also in this volume, make a similar point from a policy development point of view. They note the conceptual and practical difficulties faced by some UK policy makers in accommodating alternative approaches to the framing and delivery of sport programmes to ethnically diverse groups. In this case policy makers' own gospel was pushing them to promote assimilationist policies that would allow integrating those minority groups into the main stream sport instead of attending to their real needs and devising alternative sport policy interventions. As a result, both ethnic minorities' perceptions of sport and the policy process of designing and delivering relevant programmes become sidelined and patterns of ignorance get reinforced. Sport management scholars therefore, have a duty to promote culturally sensitive approaches to management and diverse forms of knowledge in their research and teaching.

Culture does make Sport Management Research Interesting

Culture is a powerful analytical category, which if systematically employed could help better understand any phenomenon including management. Similarly, culture does make sport management research interesting. It achieves that, not only by challenging taken for granted assumptions, but by exploring new ideas as well. By definition the purpose of sport management conceptions and practices is to facilitate people's active and passive consumption of sport and to promote positive experiences. In other words, we normally assume that sport management is charged with positive functions. However, in exploring the false dichotomy between the Occidental and Oriental, Amara & Henry submit that the normative aspect of culture and management can become a barrier to certain groups' involvement in sport. This is because the dominant management ideology has been concerned with reproducing specific cultural interpretations and experiences of sport, thus, it has been struggling to acknowledge and promote alternative modes of delivery. Consequently, the authors propose reconsidering the dominant policy view of multiculturalism. Interestingly, Apostolopoulou, Papadimitriou & Damtsiou's study in this volume, shows how mega-events, such as the Olympic Games, can evoke the same 'own' versus 'other' dichotomy in the consumption of licensed products linked to the 2004 Athens Olympics. The huge symbolic significance of the Games for the Greek's national identity was the main motivating factor behind the purchase of various products, which were considered not because of their material utilities but for their social-symbolic meaning.

Pope's personal reflective journey toward embracing and articulating a cultural contexts approach to the field of sport management provides an instructive example of what and how sport management students could do to engage with the concept and praxis of culture. More specifically, he makes it clear that the development of cultural sensitivity requires deliberate personal, theoretical, methodological and practical interventions. Maxwell & Taylor's contribution provides another example that culture can indeed make sport management research interesting. The potential of cultural diversity as a source of creativity and greater organisational effectiveness has long been established in sport management literature (Chelladurai, 2005, Doherty & Chelladurai, 1999). However, Maxwell & Taylor demonstrated the creative interplay between theory and practice using as a case in point the work of community sport organisations in Australia. In particular, unpacking multiculturalism as a social capital allows them to identify the specific mechanisms that turn cultural diversity into a positive force of social inclusion. These include the development of trust, cooperation and community networks which have significantly enhanced the work of community sport organisations. From a research point of view it is worth pointing out that the successful incorporation of Muslim minorities in community sport has become possible because their 'lay' knowledge has been acknowledged and acted upon by the main stream 'professional' workers. The work of Frisby & Millar (2002), Pitchford & Collins (2010) and Vail (2007) further supports the power of innovative sport management and culture-specific approaches to community sport, which runs counter to the main stream management wisdom. In those instances the political and production aspects of culture have played a prominent role as they necessitated reconsidering the socio-economic organisation of sport and its form of governance. Establishing a culturally sensitive community sport model requires changing the market or state-led system of delivery to more self-organising patterns of provision and non-hierarchical forms of self-governance.

Sport Management Research as a Form of Cultural Analysis

Sport management research, in its variety of approaches and units of analysis, represents a form of cultural analysis, which is both abstract in that it expresses unity of system and practice, and specific in-so-far as it is bounded to a world of beliefs and practices. Feldman (1986, p. 591) posits that "culture is context. It is the system of symbols that people use to give meaning and order to their actions and the actions of others; action is meaningful only in terms of the symbolic context in which it is interpreted". Feldman's culture-as-context approach to management strongly emphasises the role of symbolic forms including concepts, theories, plans and goals in determining what is changing in organisations. Those forms, as well as others such as sport organizations' structures, rules, policies and symbols perform an interpretative function, because they act as primary points of reference for the way people think about, and make sense of, the context in which they work. It follows that sport managers' main role becomes the management of meaning. Thus, sport management research also performs a similar function as it actively shapes the cultural framing of sport by assigning patterns of meaning to events and interactions taking place in the field. Ultimately, researchers try to explain managers' behaviour which is always determined by local symbolic systems, but they use culture in singular, or as an analytical category, to conduct the analysis.

Sport management research is a form of cultural analysis grounded in specific epistemologies, and it is the researcher's responsibility to recognise and utilise the power of this analytical tool. Sport management analyses invariably employ metaphors, models and narratives, as a tool for representing and interpreting the reality. Morgan (2006, p. 4) argues that "all theories of organisation and management are based on implicit images or metaphors that lead us to see, understand, and manage organisations in distinctive, yet partial way". It is important, however, to acknowledge that various theoretical accounts almost inevitably bear signs of the local resources that constitute them. In this regard Harding (1998, p. 61) notes that "cultural specificity could, should, and does have positive effects on the growth of knowledge". All contributions in this collection testify to the validity of the claim that sport management research represents a form of cultural analysis informed by local knowledge. Irrespective of the theoretical stance (e.g. critical multiculturalism, social capital and symbolic interaction) and methodological approach (e.g. case studies, consumer surveys, interviews and observations) of the studies they all highlight that sport management knowledge is grounded in local systems of knowledge. This is representative of the *nomos*-building aspect of culture and sport management — a constant strive to create order of chaos and to impose meaning on the world around us. The vitality of sport management research will be guaranteed by its ability to draw insights from locally meaningful practices, which have been informed by certain systems of symbols.

References

Amis, J., Slack, T., & Hinings, C.R. (2004). Strategic change and the role of interests, power and organisational capacity. *Journal of Sport Management*, *18 (2)*, 158-199.

Caza, A. (2000). Context receptivity: Innovation in an Amateur Sport Organization. *Journal of Sport Management, 14*, 227-242.

Chelladurai, P. (2005). Managing organisations for sport and physical activity: A systems perspective. Scottsdale, AZ: Hotcomb Hathaway.

Doherty, A., & Chelladurai, P. (1999). Managing cultural diversity in sport organisations: A theoretical perspective. *Journal of Sport Management, 13,* 280-297.

Feldman, S. (1986). Management in context: An essay on the relevance of culture to the understanding of organisational change. *Journal of Management Studies, 23(6)*, 587-607.

Frisby, W., & Millar, S. (2002). The actualities of doing community development to promote the inclusion of low income populations in local sport and recreation. *European Sport Management Quarterly, 3*, 209-233.

Girginov, V. & Sandanski, I. (2008). Understanding the changing nature of sports organisations in transforming societies, *Sport Management Review, 11*, 21-50.

Haas, P. (2004). When does power listen to truth? A constructivist approach to the policy process. *Journal of European Public Policy, 11(4)*, 569–592.

Harding, S. (1998). *Is Science Multicultural*? Bloomington: Indiana University Press.

Kikulis, L. (2000). Continuity and change in governance and decision making in national sport organisations: Institutional explanations. *Journal of Sport Management, 14*, 293-320.

Laurent, A. (1983). The cultural diversity of Western conceptions of management. *International Studies of Management and Organisations, XIII*, 75-96.

Morgan, G. (2006). *Images of Organisation*. London: Sage.

Nkomo, S. (1992). The emperor has no clothes: Rewriting race in organizations. *Academy of Management Review, 17(3)*, 487-513.

Nonaka, I., & Takeuchi, H. (1995). The Knowledge-Creating Company. How Japanese Companies Create the Dynamics of Innovation. Oxford: Oxford University Press.

O'Reilly, N., & Knight, P. (2007). Knowledge management best practices in national sport organizations. *International Journal of Sport Management and Marketing, 2(3)*, 264–280.

Pitchford, A., & Collins, M. (2010). Sports development as a job, career and training. In M. Collins (ed.). *Examining Sports Development* (pp. 259-289). Oxford: Routledge.

Skinner, J., Stewart, B., & Edwards, A. (1999). Amateurism to professionalism: Modelling organisational change in sport organisations, *Sport Management Review, 2*, 173-192.

Thibault, L. (2010). Trends in Sport Management as an Academic Discipline. *Keynote Paper.* European Association of Sport Management Congress, Prague, 15-19 September. 2010.

Vail, S. (2007). Community development and sport participation. *Journal of Sport Management, 21*, 571-59.

Index